MINDING BODIES

TEACHING AND LEARNING IN HIGHER EDUCATION

James M. Lang, Series Editor

A list of titles in this series appears at the end of this volume.

Minding Bodies

HOW PHYSICAL SPACE, SENSATION, AND MOVEMENT AFFECT LEARNING

Susan Hrach

West Virginia University Press · Morgantown

ISBN 978-1-949199-98-7 (cloth) / 978-1-949199-99-4 (paperback) /
978-1-952271-00-7 (ebook)

Library of Congress Cataloging-in-Publication Data

Names: Hrach, Susan, author.
Title: Minding bodies : how physical space, sensation, and movement affect
        learning / Susan Hrach.
Description: First edition. | Morgantown : West Virginia University Press,
        2021. | Series: Teaching and learning in higher education | Includes
        bibliographical references and index.
Identifiers: LCCN 2020051294 | ISBN 9781949199987 (cloth) | ISBN
        9781949199994 (paperback) | ISBN 9781952271007 (ebook)
Subjects: LCSH: Perceptual learning. | Human body in education. | Mind
        and body. | Movement, Psychology of. | Holistic education.
Classification: LCC LB1067 .H73 2021 | DDC 370.15/5—dc23
LC record available at https://lccn.loc.gov/2020051294

Book and cover design by Than Saffel / WVU Press

My mind was not parachuted in to save and supervise some otherwise helpless concoction of dumb meat.

—Guy Claxton, *Intelligence in the Flesh*

CONTENTS

....

Preface

. . . .

NO MORE BRAINS ON STICKS

. . . .

What if faculty members required students to sign the following waiver prior to enrollment in a traditional college course?

> I understand that over the next 15 weeks, this course will require me to remain seated in class for 37.5 hours, plus an anticipated requirement of 75 hours for homework, to total an anticipated 112.5 hours. Sitting for this length of time has been linked to the following adverse health outcomes, for which I will not hold responsible the instructor or the institution: anxiety, depression, heart disease, breast and colon cancer, type 2 diabetes, high blood pressure, obesity, osteoporosis, osteoarthritis, and back pain.

It may seem unfair to link these conditions directly to taking a single college course. These ailments are linked to sets of other complex factors and may only develop over decades, but the phrase "sitting is the new smoking" feels like an important twenty-first-century reckoning. The widely discussed and unanticipated epidemic of mental illness on campuses coincides with increased sedentary habits and time spent indoors, behind electronic screens. The vaunted human brain is turning out, as neuroscience probes it, to have some evolutionary vulnerabilities that can work against our well-being. We cannot deny our distance from the evolutionary physical conditions that shaped our embodied brains' expectations for continual daily movement, a natural and varied diet, and sleep patterns regulated by natural light. Our embodied brains are crying for help in "the age of the chair," as British author and academic Vybarr Cregan-Reid (2018b; see also 2019) has termed it. In the course of writing a book about how bodies impact learning, it's been impossible for me to ignore the implications of bodily health. I aim to bring the body into focus with an inclusive vision of wellness in the college classroom for bodies of all types and abilities.

This book represents a contribution to the scholarship of integration: I seek to bring the insights of embodied cognition, a subfield of neuroscience and cognitive psychology, to bear on practices of teaching and learning in college. An embodied teaching practice requires recasting cognition as a whole-body enterprise, yet faculty are typically unaccustomed to thinking about the body's role in learning at all. Discourse on well-being in higher education often focuses on belonging, flourishing, and transforming, but until the COVID-19 pandemic entered our universe, we did not routinely prioritize the physical health of students, staff, and faculty. The pandemic has dramatically demonstrated how a threat to physical health can affect every institution in a society. But preventing catastrophic illness is an extreme end of the embodied awareness spectrum. Teachers whose jobs involve nurturing brain growth should know that routine physical health impacts cognitive performance. Brains are organs of the body, with specific vulnerabilities and strengths, like any other organ or system. They do not function in isolation from circulatory systems or digestive systems or endocrine systems or even ecological systems we think of as "external." Intellectual performance demands physical energy that bodies must supply.

This book draws from the conclusions of experimental studies to recommend classroom applications, some empirically tested and some newly invented. I've used most of the exercises I describe here, and I can testify to the increase in enjoyment and engagement in learning for both me and my students. Understanding embodied cognition science has provided me with new insights for why many familiar, evidence-based practices work well, and it's challenged me to try some unorthodox and unfamiliar activities, too. After twenty years in the college classroom, my decisions about how to create learning experiences for my students are now informed by a different set of criteria than they used to be, based on how to build knowledge and skills through physical movement, an attention to the spatial environment, and a sensitivity to the energy bandwidth of my students as the term progresses.

Over the course of reading widely and far afield from my own disciplinary background—early modern literature—I have discovered surprising new ways to make sense of common experiences, both in the classroom and in my personal life. I can offer reasons informed by embodied cognition science to explain why even shy or introverted faculty may enjoy lecturing, why good ideas often seem to occur in the shower, why grief over the death of a pet can be especially intense, why a desire for in-person learning persists despite good online alternatives, and why walking barefoot in the grass can ease a rough day as quickly as bourbon on the rocks. (At the end of this book, you can test yourself by offering your own embodied cognition-based explanations for this quirky set of observations, and add some of your own.) I now regularly stumble on pieces of evidence for the inextricable interconnection between bodies and learning, like this delightful artifact tweeted by the Duke University Archives staff:

Knitters gonna knit.

(This is a passage from the April 21, 1947 meeting minutes of the Council of the Woman's Government Association. Frey is the WSGA President.)

Frey asked James if she knew of any way to prevent the students from knitting when there is an outside speaker. This is a suggestion from Dean Baldwin. The Council agreed that it was nigh to impossible. (May 17, 2018)

Busy fingers, busy brains: good thing Dean Baldwin didn't have to cope with the smartphone. To explain students' compulsion to knit, as well as your own students' relationships with their smartphones and other pertinent phenomena, I'll be introducing you to six principles of embodied cognition science. I devised these principles as a nonspecialist's guide for other nonspecialists. I've synthesized the work of scientists and science writers whose talks and publications for general audiences have been formative for my thinking. I am grateful for their clear translations of neuroscience and hope to provide the same clarity for my readers.

The seeds of this project were planted when my experiences with teaching early literature to undergraduates first started to seriously falter, I'd say around 2009. It was no longer possible to assume they would care about anything historical. "Why does this matter?" was the bewildered expression I most often read in their faces. I talked to other faculty at conferences who shared that their departments were discontinuing surveys of early literature, a concession to pure lack of interest among their students. And yet the summer study abroad programs I was fortunate to design and lead for our students produced a much different response. Walking in the footsteps of writers or even fictional characters from the past transformed the learning experience. Place-based learning worked, and after I read the pedagogical research that informs it, I understood that this wasn't just luck. I started wondering how it might be possible to bring any of that excitement into a regular classroom on campus. I suspected it had something to do with the senses, and developing a sense of empathy for human beings in the past.

In 2016 I started researching empathy in earnest, beginning with the work of Antonio Damasio, a neuroscientist whose work delves into the biological sources of emotion. Damasio's (1999) engrossing descriptions of the "as-if body loop" gave me a way to understand the effectiveness of sensory experience in place-based learning. Later, I read the work of neuroscientist Lisa Feldman Barrett (2017a), whose constructivist account of emotion led me to revise my understanding of the brain's default prediction mode. (More on this ahead in the introduction.) Eventually, my reading expanded to include not only more embodied cognition science but research on human evolutionary development, physical activity, sleep, and the effects of nature on our well-being. All of this impacted me personally as well; I began thinking of my bike commute, my yoga practice, and my amateur tennis game as directly relevant to my performance as a thinker. My writing habits started to involve a lot more standing and walking. I prioritized sleep. I paid more attention to the impact of soundscapes and natural light on my ability to feel calm and clearheaded.

Brain on a Stick. Note that the student is seated in a chair and drawn with an oversized head. (Comic by Jorge Cham. © 1997–2016 Piled Higher and Deeper, www.PhDComics.com. Originally published January 26, 2009. Used by permission.)

Humans, especially academics, tend to ignore or dismiss our bodies as locations of cognitive processing. But we are not brains on sticks, and neither are our students. As philosopher Jennifer McMahon noted in a 2019 Transformative Learning Conference session, "We Are More than Things That Think: Meditations on Embodied Learners, Learning, and Instruction," our first and last encounters with our students reflect a state of disembodiment: the class roster and the grade entry page contain lists of student names, mostly without any indication of a human presence attached. This is true in reverse as well—class schedules list only an instructor's name or the uninspiring placeholder, "Staff." Our inheritance of body/mind dualism not only makes such practices seem innocuous but reinforces perceptions of bodies as shells that can be largely ignored.

A study that investigated the effects of body/mind dualism on behavior showed that people are susceptible to making poor choices for their bodily health (like eating unhealthy food) when their perception of their bodies as mere shells has been reinforced (Forstmann et al. 2012). If one's thoughts or feelings are believed to be completely separate from one's body, taking care of physical well-being can quickly become a low priority. Using data from the National Longitudinal Study of Adolescent to Adult Health to track rates of depression as well as metabolic syndrome, a recent study found that "for minorities from disadvantaged backgrounds, finishing college pays substantial dividends for mental health, but simultaneously exacts costs with regard to physical health" (Gaydosh et al. 2018, 109). As the authors discuss, "Upwardly mobile minorities may also feel that their achieved position is tenuous. To cope with these stressors, individuals may deploy strategies that are effective in alleviating mental strife but are harmful for physical health" (112; see also Jackson et al. 2010). Classroom norms that require prolonged sitting plus a college culture that encourages poor sleep habits and junk food consumption fail to provide students with constructive tools for lifelong holistic wellness. Body/mind dualism may harm traditionally underrepresented groups disproportionately.

The norms of higher education in the United States that were formed during the twentieth century reflect an industrial ethos built on equality and standardization rather than equity. But human beings are not widgets. The students in college classrooms today need particular encouragement to persevere, and a sense from faculty that we believe in their capabilities to learn and to grow. At present, our system of higher education works best for those whose backgrounds have primed them to succeed. Rather than being an engine of opportunity, we are reproducing existing socioeconomic disparities. Whatever it is we've been doing, it's not working well for those who need it most. The American Association of Colleges and Universities, among a growing chorus of other organizations, has challenged faculty and administrators to look unflinchingly at the socioeconomic data on college graduation rates. In addition to providing tools that support our efforts to teach teamwork and problem-solving, such organizations are rightly exhorting us to find equitable ways to educate more people from across the socioeconomic spectrum.

Bringing an awareness of our physical bodies into academic endeavors makes education more humane. Whatever the differences in our cultural and socioeconomic backgrounds, our genetic predispositions, or our habits of mind, we are united by our bodies' need for sleep and by the way being hungry or thirsty can make us cranky. We are all affected by expectations (our own and those of others) that drive our perceptions of our bodies and our physical capabilities. In the course of writing this book, I have marveled at the ways we underestimate our bodies as sources of knowledge and skill. Humans are phenomenally adaptive: an acute sense of touch and hearing can allow a blind person to produce carpentry, strong and coordinated arms can allow a person without the use of their legs to play wheelchair tennis, and intense cardiovascular fitness can allow a multiple amputee to pitch hay and drive a tractor. Just as we know that a growth mindset promotes academic achievement, our health and well-being can benefit from a belief in our bodies' fundamental capacity for mobility, expressed in a diverse variety of forms. We are built to move, and maintaining or improving mobility enhances the performance of our brains.

One of the most challenging aspects of this topic has been my wish to take an inclusive and compassionate approach to limited physical mobility while encouraging readers to reject sedentary norms. The brain science is simply clear: if we want our brains to work as effectively as possible, we need to make use of whatever mobility we've got. The mind is an expression of both brain and body awareness. As neuroscientist V. S. Ramachandran has noted, "perhaps it's time to recognize that the division between mind and body may be no more than a pedagogic device for instructing medical students—and not a useful construct for understanding human health, disease, and behavior" (1998, 221). Rather than seeing bodies as yet another category for difference, our priority to create a sense of belonging in the classroom can mean emphasizing our common humanity. Dealing with the physical can offer unusual ways for us to connect with each other and take risks together as human beings. Our unfortunate but common practice of treating learners like brains on sticks (a metaphor reputedly made first by eco-philosopher Joanna Macy) resonates because it's so clearly the truth. We've created and reinforced a divide between brain and body in Western culture for hundreds of years, and in academe, our misunderstanding of thinking as a head-only process has seriously impaired our understanding of learning and practices of education. I hope it will seem shocking to us in the future that we once thought that bringing together the bodies of dozens, sometimes hundreds, of human beings only to have them sit quietly and listen for hours and weeks and years on end was the best way for them to learn. I hope we'll understand that taking good care of our bodily health and well-being are marks of our care for ourselves as thinkers.

HOW BODIES AFFECT THE LEARNING PROCESS

. . . .

Imagine the quintessential college lecture: a large room, with students in rows cascading from the back, facing a wall of chalkboards or perhaps a large screen, and the expert standing behind his podium or table. If the lecturer is animated and engaging, he likely paces back and forth on his allotted stage. A really dynamic performance might involve the expert leaving the platform to walk up and down the aisles, continuing to talk, perhaps gesturing with her arms. While in the front, she may frequently point to parts of the screen or write on the board, sometimes with great enthusiasm. If the expert knows about Eric Mazur's (1997) work, she might interrupt herself to give students a chance to turn to a neighbor and discuss the answer to a prompt. A great college lecturer often tells stories and might even move about the space in ways that help listeners to keep track of the lecture's structure. Modeled on the rhetorical appeal of this classic college lecture, the hugely popular TED Talk format features an expert who stands and moves with polished, carefully rehearsed choreography around the stage.

It's no accident that the best lectures involve pacing, gesturing, and freedom of movement for the thinker-on-view. As a reader of this book, you yourself may have had the privilege of delivering a powerful lecture—perhaps to a smaller audience, in a humbler room, with no rehearsal—and you know that the experience is physically demanding and intellectually thrilling, at least for one person in the room. There's hard evidence that the strategies Mazur and many others promote have improved outcomes by engaging students in conversation and other mental and social activity, but active learning works even better when students' bodies are engaged. If we are really serious about optimizing the brain to improve student learning, the necessary change in our practices will require significant commitment to a new way of conducting classes. "Being" in college will need to feel more like "moving" through college. My purpose here is to explain why human beings are optimized to think while moving, and to persuade you to integrate into your disciplinary teaching the insights of embodied cognition, a field of science that explores the body's role in cognitive processes.

The role of the body in the learning process deserves much more attention than it has been given by most of us in higher education. In addition to our inheritance of Cartesian body/mind dualism, we've gotten stuck in an industrial-age model for educating human beings. Like factory production, learning has been broken into various areas and linear sequences. We've organized sharply defined academic disciplines and curricula and standardized measurements to convey educational performance. At the top of the prestige heap are researchers with deep knowledge of narrow areas. The generalist's broad perspective has been devalued, despite evidence that learners who draw from a variety of experiences are better able to grasp and solve complex problems (see Epstein 2019). The same paradigm has shaped modern medicine; specialists enjoy higher prestige for deep knowledge about narrowly defined body parts and functions. But our tendency to specialize and compartmentalize has prevented us from paying much attention to intersections, and parallels, and what insights might come from stepping back to see the macro view. In medicine as well as in higher ed, a new emphasis on integrative thinking, holistic approaches, and the whole person now provides us with an opportunity to reconsider what the body has to offer the brain—and what we may have missed in assuming they were two separate things in the first place.

The field of embodied cognition draws from phenomenology and brain science to explore how the body shapes human perception. A general summary of its shared assumptions starts from the position that our brains are not in charge in the sense that we previously thought, issuing orders to various systems and parts of the body. Rather, the brain acts as a site for hosting and curating conversations; bodily organs like the heart and lungs and brain communicate and respond to each other as part of a dynamic ecosystem through a variety of channels, including electrical, hormonal, and mechanical. A wide range of signals are communicated through nerve endings in our skin, through internal organs and tissues, and through hormonal balances and the state of our immune system, each of which interact with prior knowledge and experience to produce perception (see Hohwy 2013; Barrett 2017a). Our bodies, including our heads, are in a constant state of dynamic interrelation, just like people within a society, and organisms within an environment, and stars within a galaxy. As psychologist Guy Claxton explains the interrelations of the body, "The heart beats as it does because it is listening to the rhythms and cadences of the gut and the lungs. I am as I am because I am constantly being licked into shape by the air that I breathe, the food I digest, the birdsong in the garden I can hear and the shifting quality of the relationship I have with my wife" (2015, 54). No aspect of our bodily ecosystem remains fixed, and no change takes place in isolation.

Since embodied cognition science recognizes the body as an ecosystem within other ecosystems, its specific understanding of human thought processes is challenging to describe. I've synthesized from recent work in embodied cognition six key principles to ground the scientific framework for the applications in this book. The six principles will guide relevant implications for learning, first by recognizing the role of embodied perception in cognition, and second by developing and interrogating embodied perception to inform effective classroom practices.

I. LIKE CLOUDS OR WAVES, OUR BODIES ARE IN A STATE OF CONSTANT MOTION.

There's a reason most children (and many adults) have trouble sitting still for long periods of time, and why we find it challenging to calm down the unsettled "monkey mind" when we're trying to sleep or meditate: we are made for action. The sedentary habits we've developed since the industrial age account for a tiny fraction of the ten-thousand-year span of human history; as Swedish physician and psychiatrist Anders Hansen has calculated, condensing human evolution into a twenty-four-hour period would have us becoming couch potatoes about twenty seconds before midnight:

"Evolution is lagging. Biologically, our bodies and brains are still on the savanna, and we're more hunter-gatherer than farmer. . . . We're walking out of step with our biological age—or, should I say, *we're sitting out of step*" (2016, 200–201, emphasis mine). Hansen argues for more physical activity as a prescription for anxiety and depression, for trouble with concentration and memory, and for improving creativity and focus. Backing up his claims are numerous scientific studies, as well as plenty of anecdotal experience: Apple founder Steve Jobs was known for holding walking meetings to increase productive idea-exchange. Philosophers from Diogenes to Thoreau have championed the intellectual value of a good walk, espousing the Latin maxim *solvitur ambulando* ("it is solved by walking").

But it's not just our limbs that are built for action; the mechanical movements of our muscles and bones form one set of voices in the constant cacophony of our internal systems, which include a chorus of chemicals in the blood and a symphony of electrical impulses in the nerves (see Blakeslee and Blakeslee 2007, 203–8). Because human bodily operations are never still, each of us might be more accurately considered an event—more like a cloud or a wave—than as a discrete object. Our perception of our own bodies' continuity is a psychological construct, created by our brains from repeated interactions with various systems of the body (see Seth and Tsakiris 2018); brains interpret input from internal organs and tissues (a process known as *interoception*), from external input sensed by our eyes, ears, nose, mouth, and skin (called *exteroception*), and from our limbs about the body's own spatial position and motion (*proprioception*). None of these systems operate in isolation, and they directly impact our ability to absorb new ideas and experiences: in other words, to learn. The implications of this first embodied cognition principle for teaching are enormous: how would education need to change if we addressed the primacy of physical movement (and bodily health) as fundamental to learning?

2. OUR EVER-MOVING BODIES PRIZE ENERGY EFFICIENCY.

If we're built to move, why don't we "just do it" more naturally? Thousands of years of human evolution have optimized strenuous and regular bursts of physical exertion needed to find food or escape predators by rewarding the brain with endorphins, but we are also quite able to withstand prolonged fasts because food isn't always readily available (see Ratey and Hagerman 2008, 35–56). Our systems continually monitor and adapt to changing conditions through a process known as *allostasis* (see Sterling and Eyer 1988), a method by which the body accommodates itself to everyday stresses. Significant stresses, such as childhood trauma, a toxic environment, and prolonged unhealthy behaviors, can create an *allostatic load* that leads to disease (see McEwen 2016). The ongoing or anticipated demands of our bodies, therefore, directly impact cognitive functioning by drawing on available energy reserves.

Our brains are the organs that interpret conditions and determine potential demands, which requires a careful management strategy. This strategy involves an efficient mode of operation based on prediction (see Clark 2013; Seth 2013). Rather than carefully monitoring the dynamic environment and continuously taking in scrupulously accurate information—which could exhaust our energy reserves—we rely on predicting what we expect in any given context, based on past experience and knowledge. Our predictions shape our understanding of the world and of our own bodily sensations on a moment-to-moment basis. The reason that accurate information can be so hard to circulate and that multiple eyewitnesses will swear to different accounts of an event is this: our brains are not reliable. The processes of perceiving, remembering, and making meaning are highly dependent on prior expectations that shape our attention, as well as available bodily energy.

Predictions may not be accurate representations of input, but they can be revised if we perceive enough value in expending the energy to "code" our errors (in neuroscience lingo) and remap expectations—in other words, to learn. This accounts for why it takes significant motivation to unlearn something that has been informing your predictions for a long time. Many of us can recall a song lyric we've misheard and can't seem to shake, even when we discover our embarrassing mistake. (My devout Catholic mom loved belting out "Hosanna" whenever Toto's "Rosanna" came on the radio in 1982, which my brother and I found hilarious.) For most college teachers, a reliable source of chuckles or groans is the misreading or mishearing by students of a phrase or term that is familiar to us but new to them. Learners grapple with new words by making predictions informed by words they already know; I am still mortified to recall repeatedly misnaming the novelist Zora Neale Hurston "Nora Zeale" in a college research paper. These are anecdotal pieces of evidence that demonstrate the brain's propensity to save energy by relying on predictions. The implications of this second embodied cognition principle are that we recognize the high energy demands of learning. Students will not be capable of learning and retaining new concepts with depleted reserves of bodily energy, which can be drained by emotional, social, and physical stresses (see

Verschelden 2017). How can we help students maintain or recover energy needed to learn?

3. OUR EFFICIENT BODIES ENGAGE TOOLS, TECHNOLOGIES, AND OTHER PEOPLE TO EXTEND OUR CAPACITIES.

If you've ever played a racket sport or gauged the texture of a food by touching it through the tines of a fork, you've witnessed the expansion of your *peripersonal* space. The sensory boundaries of our bodies do not end at the surface of our skin but extend a few feet around our bodies and accommodate whatever objects we are using as tools. Science writers Sandra Blakeslee and Matthew Blakeslee (2007, 4) explain it this way:

> This annexed peripersonal space is not static, like an aura. It is elastic. Like an amoeba, it expands and contracts to suit your goals and makes you master of your world. It morphs every time you put on or take off clothes, wear skis or scuba gear, or wield any tool. . . . When you drive a car your peripersonal space expands to include it, from fender to fender, from door to door, from tire to roof. As you drive you can feel the road's texture as intimately as you would through sandals. As you enter a parking garage with a low ceiling you can "feel" the nearness of your car's roof to the height barrier as if it were your own scalp.

Our bodily boundaries can be considered elastic because we are adept exploiters of our environments, including the brains and bodies of other creatures. The close physical relationships we form with animals and intimate human companions impact our biological functioning; snuggling with a pet, for example, releases oxytocin and lowers blood pressure. A horse and rider can simultaneously anticipate a jump through musculoskeletal coordination, their bodies mutually sensing the needed speed and lift. This is why the death or absence of an intimate companion, whether animal or person, can feel like a physical wound; a critical "limb" of peripersonal space is suddenly missing.

Humans and other animals don't perceive things around us with complete objectivity, but by how we think we can use them as *affordances*. The theory of affordances was first advanced in the 1960s by psychologist J. J. Gibson, who studied how visual perception is shaped by the subject's assessment of potential interaction with an object. Where I see a leather shoe, my dog sees a chew toy. A professor may view a smartphone as a distracting piece of gadgetry, while a student recognizes an emotional conduit to everyone she loves. We can also perceive other people as affordances; evolutionary efficiency has rewarded sociality in human brains, which are wired to connect. Rather than having to reproduce all knowledge, skills, and abilities in each individual brain, the capacity to use language allows humans access to lots of differently abled brains across time and space (see Harari 2015, 20–39). This is a major advantage of human sociality, and organizational studies confirm that the performance of groups small and large improves when the collective mind draws from diverse strengths.

To synthesize the principles of embodied cognition I've covered thus far: both your physical, biological condition and your access to tools and other humans, through interpersonal interactions and through culture at large, inseparably shape your mind. We can both replenish and exhaust each other through interpersonal interactions, so that holding hands with a loved one helps to lower your heart rate and being a target of road rage can cause your heart to race—not to mention that you may feel irrationally upset by a fender bender because your peripersonal space has been violated. As philosopher Matthew B. Crawford explains, "The boundary of our cognitive processes cannot be cleanly drawn at the outer surface of our skulls, or indeed of our bodies more generally. They are, in a sense, distributed in the world that we act in" (2015, 51). The boundaries between biology and culture—the old nature/nurture division—are more permeable than we think. The educational implications here involve our attention to the learning environment: the uses we make of materials, technology, and each other as affordances, and our awareness of peripersonal space in the classroom, especially when working collaboratively.

4. EACH OF US AFFECTS THE EMBODIED ECOSYSTEM OF OTHERS.

Seventeenth-century poet John Donne's words from *Devotions upon Emergent Occasions* poignantly capture this principle: "No man is an island, entire of itself; every man is a piece of the continent, a part of the main." Humans have evolved to be intensely social creatures, which makes efficient use of our brains. But for those at the lower end of the socioeconomic spectrum, everyday indignities, constant reminders of others' suspicion or even hostility to their presence, can cumulatively add up to a chronic energy imbalance, or allostatic load. The relatively poorer quality of African Americans' health, even when adjusted for income and education levels, is now being recognized by medical professionals as significantly affected by lifelong social stresses. Arline Geronimus (2013), researcher at the University of Michigan School of Public Health, has coined the term "weathering" for stress-induced wear and tear on the body. The impact of stress caused by socioeconomic disparity can be profound,

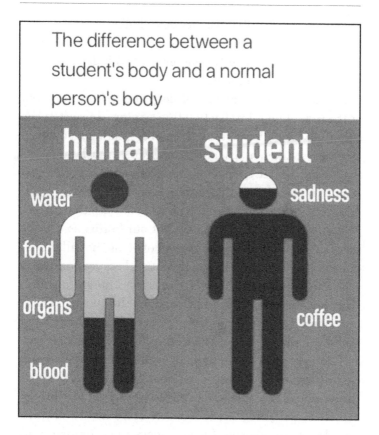

Fig. I.1. "Student Problems" wryly captures a student perspective on bodily well-being in college. (GIF by Student Problems. Social Chain. Posted December 17, 2017. https://www.facebook.com/StudentProblems/videos/1784045958388796/. Used by permission.)

resulting not only in sickness and disease but in remodeling of brain circuits and activating genetic predispositions that can be passed down for generations (see McEwen 2016; Genetic Science 2013). Or as neuroscientist Lisa Feldman Barrett (2017a, 71) sums it up, "Other people regulate your body budget too." The insights of embodied cognition explain why cognitive function is highly dependent on bodily well-being and that bodily well-being is highly dependent on a supportive environment.

Emotional stress and lack of sleep or nutrition are often at the root of poor intellectual functioning. How often has a familiar task, like answering email or grading student assignments, taken much longer and seemed much more difficult when we are tired or distracted by worry? Behavioral scientists Sendhil Mullainathan and Eldar Shafir (2013) refer to this phenomenon as a *taxed bandwidth* that affects not only our memory function but our brains' executive control: we can give the impression of being "not all there," or having poor judgment or self-control, because our bodies are struggling to provide the necessary energy to think. "If you want to understand the poor," they write, "imagine yourself with your mind elsewhere. You did not sleep much the night before. You find it hard to think clearly. Self-control feels like a challenge. You are distracted and easily perturbed. And this happens every day. On top of the other material challenges poverty brings, it also brings a mental one" (161). The root causes of a taxed bandwidth are almost impossible for strangers to recognize, and often difficult to diagnose even for ourselves, since they can range from chronic relationship stress to strain on our immune systems. If the continual activity of testing our predictions against sensory input (i.e., learning) demands bodily energy, then we must recognize that some people will have less of it to give on any particular day. The implication for teaching is that intellectual performance can vary a great deal depending on students' available bandwidth. Strategies to provide equitable environments aren't just considerate but necessary for learning. How can we support the best possible environments for learning, including behavioral and social variables?

5. KNOWLEDGE IS CONSTRUCTED THROUGH EMBODIED EXPERIENCE.

One way to prove how thoroughly the environment of our planet has shaped our bodies and minds is to see what happens when we remove ourselves from it. Astronaut Scott Kelly spent a full year on the International Space Station, and in his memoir *Endurance* (2017), Kelly writes movingly about what he missed most during his time away:

> I miss cooking. I miss chopping fresh food, the smell vegetables give up when you first slice into them. I miss the smell of unwashed skins of fruit, the sight of fresh produce piled high in grocery stores. . . . I miss the sound of people talking and laughing in another room. I miss rooms. I miss doors and door frames and the creak of wood floorboards when people walk around in old buildings. . . . I miss the sudden chill of wind on my back, the warmth of sun on my face. I miss showers. I miss running water in all its forms: washing my face, washing my hands. I miss sleeping in a bed—the feel of sheets, the heft of a comforter, the welcoming curve of a pillow. (348–49)

The things Scott Kelly missed most are physical sensations: tastes, smells, sights, sounds, and most of all, touches. His experience away from the gravitational pull of the earth and its natural elements (plants, wind, water, sun, other people) persuasively reflect the primacy of our existence as creatures of our planet. When we think, that process is deeply shaped by our physical experiences.

Our perceptions are formed by our brains through simultaneous signals from the body's various internal systems and tested against predictions made by our brains based on past experiences. What we sense is not objectively "reality" but a selective impression of reality constrained by our experiences, abilities, and needs. Hills are steeper when we're tired, or when we are very young (or old). The bus ride is longer when we're hot and exhausted. *Affective realism* is the phrase neuroscientists use to describe the way our experience of the world is always shaped by internal conditions (see Siegel et al. 2018). Interoceptive signals are indicating information about the regulation and control of the internal systems that keep us alive, so they fundamentally shape cognitive processes. As neuroscientist Anil Seth (2017, 14:31–15:33) explains, "experiences of being an embodied self are more about control and regulation than figuring out what's there. So our experiences of the world around us and ourselves within it—well, they're kinds of controlled hallucinations that have been shaped over millions of years of evolution to keep us alive in worlds full of danger and opportunity. We predict ourselves into existence. . . . We are biological, flesh-and-blood animals whose conscious experiences are shaped at all levels by the biological mechanisms that keep us alive." Although the nature of human consciousness remains a hotly contested topic in science and philosophy, neuroscientists like Seth are establishing a vital framework for the ways that our animal bodies shape our perceptions. The educational implications of this embodied theory of consciousness are complex. When we find ways for students to make use of their bodies in acquiring deep knowledge, we must then practice observing, guiding, and assessing the unfurling of their developing thoughts and understanding.

6. OUR BODIES REWARD LEARNING.
....

"If nothing else is calling on our time and energy," writes Guy Claxton (2015, 115), "we are built to be both acquisitive and inquisitive." Scholarship of teaching and learning has effectively applied neuroscience to establish the ways we acquire new knowledge—through retrieval and spaced practice, enhanced by social and emotional connection. The insights of embodied cognition explore the role of physiology in those processes. Our bodies can adjust to an environment before we're able to articulate an awareness of it: the unfurling of conscious thought often begins in the body. In experiments to test a "somatic marker hypothesis" conducted by neuroscientist Antonio Damasio (1996, 1419), participants were taught a gambling card game that required quick decision-making based on prediction. Participants' skin registered subdermal electrical activity about four seconds before they selected a card. Damasio (1416) offers this explanation: "Certain classes of situation, namely those that concern personal and social matters, are frequently linked to punishment and reward and thus to pain, pleasure, and the regulation of homeostatic states, including the part of the regulation that is expressed by emotion and feeling. The inevitability of somatic participation comes from the fact that all of these bioregulatory phenomena, including emotion, are represented via the somatosensory system." We are built to learn through an integrated system, so that physical and emotional states bear on our perception and cognition. "Emotion is never truly divorced from decision-making, even when it is channeled aside by an effort of will," as Sandra Blakeslee and Matthew Blakeslee (2007, 191) elaborate: "Even a mathematician pursuing the trail of a new proof is driven by a blend of personal ambition, curiosity, and the sometimes spine-tingling Platonic beauty of the math itself." We can't separate feelings and sensations (like tingling spines) from "rational" thought because all thinking arises from an affective state of one sort or another.

Your affective state, a reflection of your body's ecosystem, determines to a large extent how you process new information. Neuroscientists probing the mechanisms of curiosity have demonstrated that inducing and relieving curiosity stimulates activity in the brain regions associated with reward processing and enhanced memory (see Kang et al. 2009; Jepma et al. 2012). Just call us *infovores*, according to neuroscientists Irving Biederman and Edward A. Vessel (2006, 247): "It's a craving that begins with a simple preference for certain types of stimuli, then proceeds to more sophisticated levels of perception and cognition that draw on associations the brain makes with previous experiences." Learning under the right conditions, with the right balance of familiar and new information to process, appears to release endorphins to the brain's pleasure receptors. Biederman and Vessel studied the effect of various kinds of visual stimuli on the brain's opioid receptors; their work supports the hypothesis that we derive the most pleasure from being able to place a new or novel experience within the context of our memories, which make possible a rich interpretation.

The same principle explains why a lecture can be a deeply satisfying experience for those who bring to the occasion their own knowledge of the subject and thus have a handy scaffolding for hanging new information. Without that context, we need other lures to value ideas that are new. Literary scholar G. Gabrielle Starr (2013, 26) has considered the ways the sister arts of poetry, music, and visual art produce pleasure in our brains; Starr defines art as fundamentally an event, rather than an object (just like the body!), that "helps us understand a world we cannot fully predict, helps us value things that are new and learn how to compare what seems, at first, incommensurable." Art can serve as a gateway for curiosity. Once attracted to new ways of perceiving, our bodies reward us on a biochemical, physiological level for acquiring new information and encountering new situations with openness.

To recap, here are the six principles of embodied cognition I've identified as relevant to understanding how bodies impact the learning process:

1. Like clouds or waves, our bodies are in a state of constant motion.
2. Our ever-moving bodies prize efficiency.
3. Our efficient bodies engage tools, technologies, and other people to extend our capacities.
4. Each of us affects the embodied ecosystem of others.
5. Knowledge is constructed through embodied experience.
6. Our bodies reward learning.

The insights of embodied cognition theory reveal that learning is not a strictly mental effort but depends a great deal on the body's energy reserves and the learner's ability to connect affective states with openness to new information. Developing a deeper awareness of the ways embodied minds affect and are affected by other minds within social circles and cultures can make a difference in the quality of students' educational experiences and how successfully they can navigate the years-long pursuit of higher education. In addition to the hard work of acquiring knowledge, skills, and abilities in her chosen field, a typical student may be malnourished, sleep deprived, and chronically sedentary. Over the course of several years in school, a traditional-aged student is likely to weather major emotional events: the death of a grandparent, parental divorce, economic hardship, loneliness, or heartbreak. We are deluding ourselves to imagine that we can compartmentalize students' emotional and physical well-being during this years-long process to earn an academic degree. Teaching faculty can become much better at acknowledging the relevance of students' embodied experiences to their intellectual receptivity and at adopting a holistic view of the learning process.

The chapters of this book are designed to deepen your understanding of each of the principles of embodied cognition while applying the framework as a whole to learning in the college classroom. We'll consider ways to awaken students' senses and bodily awareness by attending carefully to our learning environments. First, we'll look at the spaces we've got and consider how to make the most of institutional buildings and rooms to invite curiosity and create a sense of belonging for students. Next, we'll think about outdoor spaces and why taking students outside can offer more than just a break from routine. We'll learn how and why incorporating sensory exercises allows students to develop embodied knowledge and understanding of subject matter. We'll look at ways to shake off the brain's predictive autopilot and open students' receptivity to new ideas and concepts. We'll consider how to help them better navigate the complexity of collaborative learning by increasing their self-awareness and social awareness. And finally, we'll think about how the lessons of embodied cognition can have deep personal impact as well as broad influence on the wider culture. As Patricia Owen-Smith (2017, 121) advocates in her call for contemplative practices including gentle movement and attending to bodily sensations (usefully defined and illustrated by the Center for Contemplative Mind in Society, 2015), "teachers can change the fabric of the world. Never has the call to assume this agency been more immediate and crucial than now. We are standing on the hallowed ground of the academy at a privileged moment in time. We are called to assume this power and authority in the service of our students, one another, and the planet." In our roles as professional educators, we have an obligation to model what we know—what contemporary neuroscience is establishing—about the interrelatedness of brain and body, and of body and environment.

Part One

. . . .

AWAKEN THE SENSES

Chapter One

....

OPTIMIZE THE CLASSROOM

....

Consider your least enjoyable teaching experiences: the class who seemed determined not to participate, no matter how animatedly you moved around the room or how relevant you tried to make the material; the class with a critical mass of cynics who seemed to poison the attitude of the rest; the students who continued to fill in the seats at the back and leave empty spaces anywhere near you at the front. You may have used the same strategies that worked well with other groups (maybe even in the hour right before) and chalked up the difficulty to poor group dynamics. It's hard for me to forget some of my lowest moments in the classroom: once, I discreetly excused the few "good apples" from the last day of class in an upper-level seminar and proceeded to deliver a scolding speech to the rest, writing "I don't care" in large letters on the board and explaining that this was the message they had been communicating to me all semester through their lack of engagement. A couple of them showed up in my office later to apologize. One of them cried. It was all very regrettable, on their part and on mine. One factor that seemed relevant but inescapable was the awful classroom we had been assigned that term: a basement cave with cement block walls, bad fluo-rescent lighting, and high-school-style desks with fixed writ-ing tablets screwed into the side of hard, small chairs. Other bad classes of mine have been assigned awkward rooms as well: rear entrances that invited students to stay as far as pos-sible away from the instructor, weird alcoves that became a haven for the disaffected and struggling. When I think about the pattern of all of these experiences and how frequently the physical space introduced an obstacle to productive learning, it seems obvious: human beings are unavoidably affected by our physical environments, and research confirms it.

In this chapter, I return to the six principles I identified in the introduction and consider how each concept applies to the design and use of interior learning spaces. I draw from neuroscience and apply its insights to spatial environments, sharing ideas primarily for classroom faculty but includ-ing further recommendations for campus change-makers. This is an exciting area of development in education, with wide-ranging implications for the ways we maximize both campus facilities and time, for both faculty and students. As José Antonio Bowen and C. Edward Watson (2017) remind us, the face-to-face classroom is expensive. Our value as fac-ulty members in a physical classroom—especially if we teach undergraduates—resides in our combined subject matter expertise and our skill in facilitating learning. Our impact as professionals will be limited unless we bring the second part of that equation to our work.

PRINCIPLE I: LIKE CLOUDS OR WAVES, OUR BODIES ARE IN A STATE OF CONSTANT MOTION.

We know from the principles of embodied cognition that a productive learning experience involves asking students to move—to stand if possible—as they process ideas. Because movement is integral to perception and expedites the circulation of neurochemical signals, human beings literally think better on our feet. Research on physical activity in the classroom suggests that the frontal lobe of the brain, responsible for executive control and working memory, shows increased activity when subjects are standing (see Mehta 2015), and sedentary behavior increases risk of long-term cognitive impairment (see Siddarth et al. 2018). Studies with primary school students show significant increases in cognitive function— the ability to stay on task and concentrate—when standing desks are introduced in the classroom (see Wick et al. 2018; Wendel et al. 2016). Most college classrooms, however, are built for sitting, and the most feasible solution for faculty is to create opportunities to stand or move whenever possible. Moving around the room should increase inclusiveness, so use extra care when planning activities to ensure students with limited mobility can comfortably take part. Strategies that invite or require students to stand or move around the room can include some inexpensive and simple ideas:

- Try a stand-up meeting. As an opening activity, ask students to stand and turn to face someone in front of or behind them (not the person they're sitting next to, who's likely to be known or familiar). Give them a minute or two to recall with each other what they learned in the previous class meeting. If it's their first exposure to new content, ask them to share anything they already know about the topic. These are evidence-based practices for the first five minutes of class from James M. Lang's *Small Teaching* (2016), and they're easy to adapt for getting students out of their seats.
- Direct your students to post ideas and results from individual or group work on whiteboards, flip charts, or giant sticky

sheets on the walls. Covering walls with students' own hand-
writing transforms an impersonal, multi-use room to a space
with their own literal imprint.

- If your furniture allows rearrangement, invite students to
  help set up the classroom—moving tables and chairs, raising or lowering blinds as needed for the day's activity—and
  reset the room at the end of class, which allows students to
  own the learning environment. Even significant alterations
  to a room can be accomplished quickly when lots of people
  are working together, and physical activity raises students'
  energy levels for the start of your class.

Barring pandemic conditions, touching the furniture, the
windows, the boards, the podium, and the room's available
technology offers students an opportunity to explore the
space with their own hands, become intimately familiar
with these objects, and thus inhabit the classroom more
comfortably. Some students may need encouragement to
overcome a resistance to physical movement, and we should
be prepared to explain why moving around improves their
ability to learn. Transparency about how movement improves thinking can increase students' willingness to try.

For Campus Change-Makers
....

Classrooms designed to maximize density by tightly pack-
ing in desks or pinning students into rows present a real
challenge for mobility and thus learning. Space is costly on
a college campus, but this issue gets straight to the heart of
our mission: if we want better learning experiences and improved learning outcomes in higher education, then space for
students to move around as they think (stand, turn, face different directions, occupy various areas of the room) becomes

a necessary investment. Shaping spaces to accommodate students with limited individual mobility will benefit all learners by improving the flow of movement, following a principle of universal design that recommends designs that "can be used efficiently and comfortably and with a minimum of fatigue" (National Disability Authority 2014). The challenges to our conventional interior spaces and our traditional modes of delivery in higher ed are significant: moving around during class hasn't been the norm. In this particular realm, faculty practitioners have not been at the forefront of innovation. Interior designers are shaping the future of educational spaces, and their work is both informed by and contributing to research on how the environment impacts learning.

As universities gradually renovate older classrooms and libraries with mobile furniture to foster creativity and collaboration, workplaces are quickly transforming into flexible office spaces that encourage innovation. The accelerating movement to design spaces for the information age is supported by the science of embodied cognition. Variety in environmental settings helps to stimulate the brain: "By making no two common spaces, landscaped areas, or offices, alike, the mind is awakened by new experiences," explains the cutting-edge design firm NBBJ, hired by Amazon to build its Seattle headquarters. NBBJ followed this practice after consulting with neuroscientists about how the brain responds to variety in physical environments (Levy 2017). Researchers are teasing apart concepts like privacy and attentional focus to tailor the design of offices for specific work cultures and functions. It's possible to support both solitude and collaboration, but the balance can be critical and site-specific (see Congdon et al. 2014). Knowledge economy workplaces are dedicating significant resources to designing spaces for optimal human interaction and cognitive performance, and universities stand to benefit from these insights as well.

One boost in classroom design research has been financed by Steelcase Inc. through its Active Learning Center Grants. Beginning in 2015, Steelcase began funding proposals for classroom renovations, selecting institutions at secondary and postsecondary levels of education with the expectation that grant recipients conduct studies on how the renovated spaces affect learning. Research results suggest that not only do students and faculty prefer classrooms that encourage mobility, but they show measurable improvements in behaviors that support learning. Students reported statistically significant improvements on commonly identified factors, including "better, more frequent interactions"; "more active, hands-on experiences"; and "greater participation, motivation, and focus" (Steelcase, "Active Learning Centers," 4–5). Having students move around also improves their comprehension and retention of material in subjects that require spatial reasoning (see Jaeger et al. 2016; Holton 2010). Spaces that allow physical mobility create a ripple effect: by improving the focus and clarity of individual students' thinking and by making it possible to connect more easily with classmates and the instructor, the classroom design promotes engagement and understanding.

The single largest and most consistent change from traditional to active learning classrooms as reported by students in the Steelcase research and others involved an increase in physical movement made possible by mobile furniture configurations (see Scott-Webber 2013, 34; Steelcase, "Effects," 6–7). "Many grant recipients," reports the Steelcase research summary ("Active Learning Centers," 6), "indicated that mobility and options afforded by the ALC [Active Learning Center] classroom supported ongoing changes to pedagogy. The Ohio State University reported that its educators are *"adopting 'movement' as a pedagogy change in and of itself"* (emphasis mine). As the authors of an independent study at Iowa State University affirm, the room itself can lend itself to more creative teaching strategies: "The flexible, open design of the ALC allowed for movement within the classroom, encouraging social interaction among peers and students and instructors. Participants reported that frequent social interaction enabled students to connect with each other and their instructor to share, distribute, and co-construct knowledge, resulting in a feeling of community and engagement" (Rands and Gansemer-Topf 2017, 29). While interior design can inherently encourage more creative pedagogy, researchers recommend that faculty make use of these spaces through targeted development activities: reading books and articles on active learning strategies, participating in faculty learning communities, working together with a faculty developer as a learning spaces consultant.

PRINCIPLE 2: OUR EVER-MOVING BODIES PRIZE EFFICIENCY.

Because our brains prefer to conserve energy by predicting what might happen within a known context, a traditional classroom (seats all facing the same direction, with a screen or board or a lectern at the front) forces students to intentionally exert more energy to overcome educational inertia. Even if students have experienced lively and stimulating school environments in K–12 settings, our cultural images of school at every level predict and reinforce a conventionally passive arrangement; Ben Stein's parody of a high school teacher ("anyone, anyone?") in *Ferris Bueller's Day Off* (1986) still resonates with YouTube viewers. If an environment conforms to prior expectations (school equals sitting still and being quiet), the brain is more likely to shift into autopilot about what it thinks it's hearing or seeing. That leads to misunderstandings and difficulties with revising previously held beliefs. A well-designed learning space can encourage students to attend to the moment by disrupting their expectations for a classroom setting.

The same principle argues for mixing it up with your classroom activities. How many ways can a room be used? Would it be possible to get students out of it, even briefly, for a change of scene? The brain's response to variety suggests that no single classroom strategy needs to be verboten—take heart, skilled lecturers—but there's a good reason to avoid monotony and to engage the body whenever possible. Just as Universal Design for Learning principles provide improved access to materials for all learners, not just those with visual impairments, a learning environment based on the principles of embodied design offers learners a multiplicity of strategies to learn by using their bodies (Abrahamson 2009; Van Rompay et al. 2005). Students can pursue meaningful learning through a mix of embodied design activities, as outlined by researchers Ianes, Cramerotti, and Cattoni (2017, 33) on embodied cognition in special education:

- Adopt the lab or studio model: "Students should use their senses to reflect on stimuli, and their properties, and to perform new actions. Figurative, iconic and graphical representations should be preferred to symbolic and abstract stimuli, at least in the initial phase." Show and tell by giving students an experience with the material before talking about what it means or how it works.

- Find a space that permits free movement and exploration of tools: "All of the activities should take place in an environment without barriers, so that any action—from the bending of a finger to a body pirouette—is not hindered and can elicit feedback loops; the learning environment should also include different artefacts and different media." What counts as a "tool" in your classroom? (More on this in the next section.)

- Participate in and model physical movement: "Students should be guided, with physical cueing and teachers' feedback, in the movements that elicit conceptual insights, movements that do not always occur naturally." If you find certain gestures useful to depict an idea, get everyone involved in mirroring your demonstration. The act of hand-raising performs an important role in communicating that we are engaged and visible; ask for a show of hands in sets of questions that will involve everyone.

It might be that every day won't involve embodied learning in your course, but you can aim for mixing up lecture and discussion with physical activity: send students out for a walk, in pairs or threes, to answer a conceptual question; form teams to debate various positions from opposing sides of the room; conduct role-playing games or exercises. Find ways to use a variety of places for typically passive strategies: deliver a lecture or watch a film in a special location, like the campus museum. Arrange an on-campus field trip to a gallery, library, archive, or outreach centers students might not otherwise visit. Are there spaces at your institution that you yourself are curious to explore and would allow you to disrupt your own predictive habits shaped by the traditional classroom?

PRINCIPLE 3: OUR EFFICIENT BODIES ENGAGE TOOLS, TECHNOLOGIES, AND OTHER PEOPLE TO EXTEND OUR CAPACITIES.

Philosopher and cognitive scientist David Chalmers recounts what he noticed about his mental processes within the first month after buying an iPhone:

> The iPhone has already taken over some of the central functions of my brain. It has replaced part of my memory, storing phone numbers and addresses that I once would have taxed my brain with. It harbors my desires: I call up a memo with the names of my favorite dishes when I need to order at a local restaurant. I use it to calculate, when I need to figure out bills and tips. It is a tremendous resource in an argument, with Google ever present to help settle disputes. I can make plans with it, using its calendar to help determine what I can and can't do in the coming months. I even daydream on the iPhone, idly calling up words and images when my concentration slips. (quoted in Clark 2008, iv)

The iPhone is an affordance par excellence. We could add to the brain functions that Chalmers enumerates the smart phone's ability to magically conjure up the presence of friends, family, acquaintances, and strangers. Not limited to our own imaginations, we can see their images and hear their live voices almost at will, by lightly touching a screen. Small wonder that our handheld devices have become extensions of our bodies and have unquestionably affected every kind of interpersonal interaction.

Affordances are objects or environments that we perceive as useful tools. Technology might be game changing, but it's not an affordance until we can do something with it. Our perceptions of an object's usefulness depend furthermore on context: my older iPhone is now a homely and unreliable vessel for streaming music in the kitchen, and even a brand new one has limited value when I travel to places with spotty cellular service and no Wi-Fi. Broadly defined, technological affordances include not only smartphones and computers, but books, paper, and writing implements, chalk and chalkboards, and any other object that allows us to offload our cognitive or physical demands. But affordances are not limited to technology or even to objects; the Iowa State case study identifies affordances as environments that enable or constrain engagement: for example, "movable chairs afford students the ability to group closer together for collaborative work or discussion" (Rands and Gansemer-Topf 2017, 27). To maximize other people's brains as affordances, a learning space cultivates a sense of social belonging and promotes productive circulation among all of the learners and gives students close access to their instructor. The trick for college learning affordances, whether objects or environments, is to cultivate tools our students can use for learning and to remove prospective obstacles to them. The ongoing conversation about how to deal with smartphones and laptops in the classroom can be summarized pretty simply this way: some faculty seek ways to use devices as affordances for learning, and some faculty seek ways to prevent them from obstructing learning. Depending on the context, both kinds of strategies are important for creating productive learning environments. The same tool can be an affordance or an obstacle, and it's our job to figure out how and when it becomes either.

The magical properties of the smartphone to conjure up other human beings means that we can access other humans

Fig. 1.1. The smartphone: affordance extraordinaire, extension of self. (Personal photograph of my dog, screen wallpaper designed by my daughter, seated in a gift from friends, 2015.)

for useful information (via Wikipedia, say, or peer-reviewed publications online), but we are also distracted by a compelling interest in knowing who replied to our group text about dinner plans. As Guy Claxton (2015, 210) explains, "Our bodies are in a state of continual resonance with those around us," which includes not only those physically present but "those that we may be remembering or imagining." If we need students to engage with the human beings in the room, it seems useful to classify their smartphones as temporary obstacles, and to encourage them to set these aside. Given that phones are frequently an extension of students' peripersonal space, special treatment may be necessary; my colleague, community geographer Amanda Rees, creates "nap mats" for students to place their phones, screen down, in the center of group tables.

PRINCIPLE 4: EACH OF US AFFECTS THE EMBODIED ECOSYSTEM OF OTHERS.

Being able to move our chairs closer together affords human beings an opportunity to engage in interaction, but interpersonal communication can be exceptionally complex. How much attention do we pay to the postures of students working in groups or the ways the furniture promotes or inhibits productive relationships? Humans are acutely sensitive to the presence of other humans, and we read body language fluently. In one seminal study, actors were wired with small lights attached at seven key locations on their bodies; viewers in dark rooms were able to detect from the movement of the body lights which actors were male or female, cultural foreigners or cultural familiars, and were able to identify a range of basic emotions (happy, sad, afraid, disgusted, embarrassed) as enacted by body language alone (see Johansson

1973). A learner takes in all of that information about class-mates and makes predictions about how others will behave based on prior personal experience—which could be helpful or harmful to the interaction. Spatial zones further affect our ability to effectively interact and are culturally deter-mined; for many Americans, "personal" zones are assumed to exist between eighteen inches and four feet—generally corresponding with peripersonal space—while a "social" zone requires between four and twelve feet between individ-uals (see Blakeslee and Blakeslee 2007, 128). What kinds of interactions are we facilitating via furniture arrangements, and can we raise students' self-awareness by asking them to reflect on how changing postures or spatial distance affects their interaction? (I'll return to these questions in chapter 5, "Move around Together.")

Our interaction with other people can significantly affect our response to new ideas and experiences. Sharing new experiences together can be a bonding strategy for couples, families, and friends, and the same holds true for classes where genuine learning experiences take place. When plan-ning our expensive time in class together, faculty should consider what aspects of the material we could elicit for a group aha moment. Surprise works: multiple studies have shown that regions of the brain that affect memory reten-tion and pleasure are neurochemically rewarded when we encounter something novel (see Bischoff-Grethe et al. 2001; Fenker and Schütze 2008). Research on epistemic curiosity suggests that seeking the solution to a puzzle or mystery boosts the impact and memory retention of material (see Kang et al. 2009; Gruber et al. 2014). For example, when I screen a foreign film with students, we take breaks at criti-cal junctures to stand up and stretch, to share impressions, and to speculate about what we expect to happen next. By "chunking" novel and culturally complex material, we create an experience together. That helps not only to clear up genuine confusion but also to develop curiosity and empathy for diverse responses to sometimes surprising and difficult human dilemmas, actions, and behaviors. The film screening becomes a humanities lab.

Ideally, our embodied ecosystem extends beyond the classroom. Multiple studies over the past decade-plus have established that positive mentoring relationships with faculty members are critical to student success. These relationships can sometimes be formed in the moments before and after class, but lasting connections are built on sustained interactions and changes of scene: student organization meetings, field trips, study abroad. Office hours can provide another opportunity to build relationships, but there's a big hurdle for many students to overcome in meeting us in these spaces. As higher education trends analyst Jeffrey Selingo (2018, 3–4) writes in "The Future of the Faculty Office," "The problem with conventional office hours is that they are passive—professors wait for students to come to them. Much as teaching on many campuses has been transformed with active-learning techniques, so too must faculty-student interactions change, and that starts with designing better spaces for students and professors to meet." It's not hard to appreciate why our isolated office hallways, with doors mostly closed, are not welcoming for students, who may feel like intruders in our territory. And that's among the most privileged of our ranks, who even have private offices. Our chances to develop supportive relationships with students improve if we meet in alternative spaces, like libraries, learning commons spaces, campus cafés, or even the student recreation center. But why limit ourselves to seated environments? Perhaps the best alternative to office hours would be a standard walking circuit;

inviting students for a walk-and-talk at the rec center or around campus pathways allows us to build as well as model a healthy relationship practice.

PRINCIPLE 5: KNOWLEDGE IS CONSTRUCTED THROUGH EMBODIED EXPERIENCE.

The tradition of the grand library reading room offers an excellent example of the way environments shape our learning experiences. The central reading rooms of the U.S. Library of Congress, the New York Public Library, the University of Oxford's Radcliffe Camera, and many other university libraries feature cathedral ceilings, tall windows that allow natural light, and surrounding walls of hardwood shelves, filled with books made of paper and cloth. The colors of the rooms are earth toned, as are most of the materials contained within. Designers of these grand spaces intuitively understood what science is now proving: that furniture, colors, ceiling heights, light, and air all have an impact on our affective states. Research on the impact of color and light on brain activity and mood has demonstrated that "saturated blue" (like the daytime sky) keeps us feeling alert, and that natural light in indoor spaces helps us to maintain our circadian rhythms (see ISE 2017; Figueiro 2016). Painted to look like the sky, the ceiling frescoes in the Rose Reading Room of the New York Public Library implicitly assist patrons to work productively. In addition to color and light, the height of the ceiling itself can evoke a sense of freedom that in turn promotes relational processing, or "elaborating freely or uninhibitedly on multiple pieces of data so as to discern commonalities or higher-order abstract points of intersection" (Meyers-Levy and Zhu 2007). The room in which we're thinking facilitates the kind of thinking we do.

Fig. 1.2. The ceiling of the New York Public Library Rose Reading Room facilitates thinking about abstract connections. (Photograph courtesy of Michael M. S. Posted on Flickr, photo 078 from New York City Day Trip album, May 16, 2014. CC-BY 2.0 license.)

The atmosphere created by dozens of human beings occupying such spaces, quietly reading, typing on laptops, writing in notebooks, can be a stimulus to learning. Being in a room with lots of other engaged people provides a model for contemplating, absorbing, and wrestling with ideas in communal solitude.

As social creatures, we learn from our environment first by noticing—with mindful attentiveness—then by imitating others' behavior, then by practicing the behavior ourselves (see Claxton 2015, 234–38). Each of these steps require that the body be actively engaged. Even the first step of noticing, or learning to see, is impossible to master without the ability to move around. Our eyes depend on locomotion in order to perceive in three dimensions. "Learning to see," as philosopher Matthew B. Crawford (2015, 262n4) describes it, "means mastering the pattern of sensorimotor contingencies by which reflected light maps, in a necessary and law-like way, onto the physical objects that we encounter. . . . Mastering these patterns, which we do as infants, depends on the ability to move around, just as fingers must move around to perceive by touch." Physical exploration is necessary to notice our environment, with our eyes as well as our hands. Manually exploring the shelves of the library, for example, can teach students to notice how disciplinary knowledge has been organized, what specific topics have been treated by other humans in the past, and how our interest in various topics has changed over time. As we notice, we move not only through space but through time, adding a fourth dimension to our perception of the world. Crawford (2015, 263n5) suggests that our movement through time can deepen understanding: "If self-motion is necessary to apprehend the world, this fits with our common intuition that wisdom is impossible without biography, that is, a self that moves or changes through time and thereby 'gains perspective.' " Noticing over time fosters knowledge through repeated experiences, specifically with mindful attention to new input.

Long experience to build up the brain's predictive knowledge can be valuable, but this default prediction mode also dulls our attention. In order to open up the brain's most attentive, mindful state, we need to overcome its customary predictive habits, which is no easy task. In *How to Change Your Mind* (2018), Michael Pollan explores the potential use of psychedelic drugs in order to access the brain's most attentive, open condition. Pollan cites the research of Robin Carhart-Harris's lab at Imperial College London, which has tested the ability of LSD and other hallucinatory drugs to take our default mode network offline. Psychedelics, they suspect, "might shake people out of their usual patterns of thought—'lubricate cognition' in Carhart-Harris's words—in ways that might enhance well-being, make us more open and boost creativity" (328). These treatments show promise for people whose predictive networks have become so rigid that they produce illness (like obsessive-compulsive disorder and schizophrenia). But can we enable openness short of providing an LSD trip for our students?

An open, alert, sensitive state is necessary for attentive imitating and practicing, as well as for noticing. Imitating involves risking failure in front of others, as anyone learning a new language can attest; I witness this every time I ask students to read Shakespeare aloud or to use new terminology. Practicing is more efficient when it's done with focused attention; rote repetition is not as effective for deep learning and may even be harmful by reinforcing incorrect effort. An attentive and safe environment is therefore crucial for learning. Two kinds of embodied activities can encourage an open state: mindful meditation and play. The work of Richard J. Davidson and many others in contemplative learning has shown that even a short course of mindful meditation can impact self-awareness, attention span, and social intuition (Davidson and Begley 2012, 224; Cavanagh et al. 2019). Patricia Owen-Smith (2018) offers numerous ideas for introducing meditative practices in the classroom, including making time for intentional silence. I can recommend from my own practice two brief activities; these offer students a chance to transition from their hectic rush to class into a more calm and alert readiness for learning:

- Lead students through a series of three-way neck stretches, combined with deep breathing, noticing and releasing tension in commonly stiff areas (many demonstrations available on YouTube).
- Invite students to participate in a short, three-minute body scan exercise, which calls attention to each part of the body and invites us to notice feelings and sensations, and to relax tight areas (transcript and audio available online through University of California–Berkeley's Greater Good Science Center site).

In addition to enabling a more open mental state during class time, these activities are easy for students to repeat on their own.

Play is a second method for encouraging openness. While meditation focuses on interior, individual states, a playful environment is deeply participatory. "The play environment is the classroom by which we learn to be empathic with our fellow human beings," writes philosopher Jeremy Rifkin (2009, 94); "it is where we exercise our imagination by placing ourselves in other personas, roles, and contexts, and try to feel, think, and behave as we believe they would." Imagining others' experiences and perspectives requires curiosity and creativity, which may also facilitate the welling up of consciousness to produce new knowledge. Creative play taps into the early, unfurling stages of consciousness; the process of learning suggests that human beings are naturally makers and doers first, while understanding comes later (see Claxton 2015, 182 and 234).

Play in the higher education classroom has been developing in myriad ways over the past decade, from borrowing acting classes' warm-up and improvisation activities to pursuing historical role-play through *Reacting to the Past* games. As *Reacting* founder Mark Carnes (2014, 77) describes about the appeal and effectiveness of academic play, some students report that they enjoy the competition, some the absurdity, and some the imaginative reach: "Becoming other people was fun—researching their lives, writing papers from their perspectives, voicing their ideas in class." Noticing, imitating, and practicing through physical play can offer our best stimulus to a budding consciousness. Stephanie Briggs's (2018) online site *Be.Still.Move* offers videos and resources to support arts-based learning through movement, such as an activity that asks students to physically embody an elder relative in their family. Because knowledge is constructed through embodied experience, we're learning even as we watch others learn. It works in the communal solitude of a grand library reading room, and it's being tested in newly designed glass-walled study rooms, through which we can see others learning.

PRINCIPLE 6: OUR BODIES REWARD LEARNING.

Clinical psychiatrist John Ratey (2014, 27) argues that humans developed our large brains in tandem with our rare

Fig. 1.3. Georgia Tech's Glenn + Towers active learning and study rooms allow students to view others learning. (Photograph by Jonathan Hillyer. © 2018 Project design by VMDO Architects. Used by permission.)

abilities to move in complex ways: "The evolution of our unique brains was locked into the evolution of our wide range of movement. Mental and physical agility run on the same track." We admire the powerful speed of the jaguar, the graceful arc of an eagle, the intricate synchrony of fish swimming in schools; these animals have perfected a limited range of movements. We are the only species with an ever-expanding catalog of Olympic events. Even our youngest fellow humans can normally roll, sit, crawl, walk, dance, run, and jump. We're "the Swiss Army knives of motion," as Ratey (26) memorably puts it. Our brains work optimally when we are stimulating new cell growth, which takes place by regulating and balancing neurotransmitters (like serotonin, norepinephrine, and dopamine) and then fertilizing our new synaptic connections with neurotrophins (like brain-derived neurotrophic factor, a nerve growth agent); all of these processes are promoted by physical exercise. Ratey (2008, 55–56) suggests that the best kinds of physical exercise for learning are activities that push us to work hard while simultaneously figuring out how to move: "The more complex the movements, the more complex the synaptic connections. And even though these circuits are created through movement, they can be recruited by other areas and used for thinking. This is why learning how to play the piano makes it easier for kids to learn math. The pre-frontal cortex will co-opt the mental power of the physical skills and apply it to other situations." If activities like dance, racket sports, martial arts, and gymnastics offer the biggest bang for our brains, any kind of physical movement (like playing a musical instrument) taps into our natural learning abilities. Psychologist Peter Lovatt's research has shown that improvisational, unplanned movement facilitates creative, divergent modes of thinking; calculation and recall improve when accompanied by patterned movements, like line dances (Lewis and Lovatt 2013). Depending on the kind of thinking you want to encourage on a given day, students can enjoy a natural boost from shaking things loose or from performing a short sequence of claps or steps together.

For Campus Change-Makers

We evolved to learn through a variety of motions, so it makes sense that we respond to diversity in our learning environments as well. There's no single best kind of space, therefore, but a variety of spaces for a variety of needs. Based on his experiences watching hybrid learning spaces develop at Georgia Tech, Jeff Selingo predicts, "What we're going to see in the place [of the large college lecture hall] are physical spaces where people come together—to work on problems together, to do some teamwork exercises, or just to socialize—in a way that they're not able to do online" (quoted in Steelcase, "Tomorrow's Classroom" podcast, 13:32–14:04). Indoor spaces at universities are morphing from industrial-age uniformity in classrooms and offices to twenty-first-century multifunctional operation centers.

To return to the major themes of this chapter, classrooms ideally work as affordances for learning: they keep us alert and attentive and facilitate different kinds of productive interaction, as well as for contemplative reflection. How do your current spaces stack up? Jeanne L. Narum, principal at Learning Spaces Collaboratory, has developed a five-part list to consult when performing an audit of your learning environments, including some suggested no- or low-cost quick fixes. Narum's "Questions Relevant to Renovation" (2011, 2) includes these queries related to embodied cognition science:

- What would elevate an existing space to become a "brain-changing" space?
- What reorganization of a current space would dissolve boundaries between lecture and lab, between on-site and virtual communities?
- What can be taken out of a space to make it a better space for learning? How can the learner be given ownership of his/her space for learning?
- What possibilities exist to make every space on campus a learning space?

In the spirit of Narum's "Quick Fixes," here are some final no-cost or low-cost ideas that optimize spaces for learning:

- As the default setting for classroom window treatments, keep blinds open for natural light.

- Display posters of diverse groups of people working together and nature photographs of local landscapes in rooms where there are few windows.
- Make visible ongoing and real-time learning: display student artifacts, remove barriers from windows into labs and studios.
- Provide portable whiteboards, smaller sizes on wall hooks and larger sizes mounted on wheels, for as many classrooms as possible.
- Advocate for and promote spaces that allow movement for group work, collaboration, and communication.

Chapter Two

. . . .

TAKE IT OUTSIDE

. . . .

There's something inspiring about seeing students lounging on a grassy quad, engaged with faculty and each other in mind-expanding conversations; that idealized image is a perennial favorite for campus publications. Appealing as it is, taking students outside for class generally serves as a rare treat for a fine day or a special field trip excursion. Unless we're in the natural sciences and spend class time outdoors as a regular practice, going outside entails a pedagogical gamble. There's no guarantee of a successful learning occasion, even when students seem enthused about breaking out of the building. Because leaving the classroom is such an atypical practice, I want to begin with a cautionary tale. Even a carefully arranged experience, like a study abroad outing to the Royal Observatory in Greenwich for a discussion of the longitude problem, may fail to elicit appreciation or wonder, as happened to my colleague, mathematician Cindy Ticknor (personal communication, 2018):

I thought my plan for our Greenwich field trip would be perfect. I had everyone pack a lunch and took a lightweight sheet to spread on the grassy hillside that led up to the famous Royal Observatory. Although I wished it was under a starry night, it was a beautiful setting, looking out over London, to hear one of the students report on John Harrison, who famously solved the Longitude Problem with his chronometer. The group was composed of math-enthusiasts. What could go wrong? But no one seemed very engaged, as they leaned back, looking around. No questions arose, no big discussion resulted.

Disappointing and shallow discussions might be one of the most common experiences of college faculty, and it's especially frustrating when you've gone to great lengths to create a memorable learning event. But a number of identifiable factors may have influenced these Royal Observatory visitors' underwhelming response: limited physical or emotional bandwidth on that day (jet lag, homesickness), underdeveloped prior knowledge, or a less-than-immediate sense of relevance to connect with John Harrison and the problem of longitude. As Ticknor reflects about what she'd have done differently: "I would have prepared more reflective questions about the space and history, such as, 'Could you imagine being championed by the famous astronomer, walking up this hill to meet with him?' "

Another significant factor in these students' response may have been a sense of dislocation about the experience of a math class picnic. Spaces affect the way we behave in them—not only, as we saw in the last chapter, because our bodies respond to the properties of a room's light, and proportions, and furnishings, and fellow inhabitants but because our predictive brains bring experiences that govern what sorts of behavior feel normal in such a place. Classrooms are places where serious events and phenomena are supplied with abstract concepts that give them meaning.

The experience we bring to a traditional classroom may lull us into a state of inattention, but at least we expect to be dealing with ideas in such a room. Unless one's family or social circle conducted serious conversations about ideas at home or in the car or on walks outside, the only place a person may bring experience of talking about ideas could be a traditional classroom. There's a good reason it can feel weird to ask for thoughts on the assigned reading as others stroll past on the sidewalk and birds chirp nearby. Violating an academic norm is a real obstacle we must address to make going outside truly effective.

Flies, mosquitoes, wasps, bees, ants, spiders, allergy season, sunburn, and other realities present threats serious enough to keep some people from going outdoors much. Our impromptu vision of an intellectual idyll might be met with less-than-enthusiastic responses from students: there are bugs on the grass! I didn't dress for this! Increasingly urbanized and indoorsy human beings are less likely than ever to have spent considerable time in nature and must sometimes overcome a serious resistance, if not a phobia, to the outdoors. The term *biophobia* signals a fear and aversion to nature, while *ecophobia*, according to the environmental consulting firm Terrapin Bright Green (2014), describes "an unreasonable but deeply conditioned disgust for or reaction against natural forms or places." Like other phobias, however, both of these can be transformed through education into experiences of "curiosity, exhilaration, and even a type of mind-body systems recalibration" (17). As Penn State ecologist Chris Uhl and educational researcher Dana Stuchul (2011, 159) note, "The first step is to let go of the crippling conditioning that would have us accept living within indoor boxes as normal." The projection screen or whiteboard doesn't need to dominate our pedagogy; creative faculty have turned lightweight plastic or paper trash bags into writing surfaces that can later serve as needed receptacles for collecting litter. The insights of embodied cognition would argue that taking students outside—revising expectations about behavioral norms and helping students overcome learned aversions to the natural world—is an effort well worth planning and pursuing.

Anticipating the neuroscience that would inform embodied cognition work, linguist Mark Johnson (1987, 207) recognized the central importance of our "external" worlds on shaping mental concepts: "The environment as a whole is as much a part of the identity of the organism as anything 'internal' to the organism." Our cognitive networks, including the brain and the systems that regulate internal processes, form a bodily ecosystem that functions within other ecosystems: our social relationships, our homes, our campuses, our geographic regions. And as I've established here, the boundary line between the "inside" and "outside" of our physical bodies is more permeable than we think. Affordances allow us to sense things through objects we use as tools, for example, and the presence of certain other people can change the rate of our heartbeats. Considering that the vast majority of human evolution took place prior to industrialization, it makes sense that we are biologically wired to prefer natural environments, even specific kinds of natural features that support our survival and well-being.

The concept of biophilia, coined by psychologist Erich Fromm in *The Heart of Man* (1964) and popularized by sociobiologist E. O. Wilson in *Biophilia* (1984), expresses the idea that we are innately drawn to affiliate with other forms of life—including plants and animals—and with the natural environment of our shared planet. Neurologist Oliver Sacks (2019) testified to the remarkable transformation many of his patients suffering degenerative diseases achieved from spending time in nature:

> In 40 years of medical practice, I have found only two types of non-pharmaceutical "therapy" to be vitally important for patients with chronic neurological diseases: music and gardens. . . . The role that nature plays in health and healing becomes even more critical for people working long days in windowless offices, for those living in city neighborhoods without access to green spaces, for children in city schools or for those in institutional settings such as nursing homes. The effects of nature's qualities on health are not only spiritual and emotional but physical and neurological. I have no doubt that they reflect deep changes in the brain's physiology, and perhaps even its structure.

Biophilic design principles have drawn from scientific studies on human stress reduction, cognitive performance, and emotion, mood, and innate preference to identify the specific ways we can create built environments to mimic our ideal natural spaces. As science writer Florence Williams (2017, 127) notes in *The Nature Fix*, "Educators are scrambling to come up with [biophilic] solutions, including installing full-spectrum indoor lights and glass ceilings over classrooms." But as Williams advocates, we might try something entirely simpler: going outside.

In the introduction to this book, I identified a number of specific implications raised by applying the insights of embodied cognition to learning in higher education. For example, we know that human beings are vulnerable to the taxed bandwidth phenomenon, in which available cognitive capacity and degree of executive control are diminished by sleep and nutritional deficits, anxiety about relationships or resources, or compromised immune systems. So that implicates us in considering ways we might help our students to maintain or recover energy needed to learn and support the best possible environments for their overall health. If we care about their learning, we have a stake in harnessing the power of students' biochemical reward systems for acquiring new information and encountering new situations with openness and curiosity. And our stake in their learning means we will be more effective by figuring out how to observe, guide, and assess the unfurling of students' developing thoughts and understanding—as expressed by/within their bodies. Each of these complicated challenges, along with creating variety and encouraging movement as part of the learning process, can be addressed by going outside.

Faculty members at the University of Virginia's School of Architecture have advocated for a paradigm that would help people to see time spent outdoors as a critical component of health. The nature pyramid, a concept attributed to Tanya Denckla-Cobb and further developed by Tim Beatley (2012), uses the familiar concept of the food pyramid to show the frequency and diversity of outdoor experiences we should seek out as a prescription for healthy living. Beatley, who heads the Biophilic Cities Project, incorporates in the pyramid geographic range (local to global) as well as the frequency, duration, and intensity of immersion experiences. I'd like to apply the concept of the nature pyramid here to envision ways that we can design academic experiences that correspond to each level of immersion. Moving from the pyramid's peak (least frequent, geographically distant, most immersive) kinds of experiences to its base (daily, the most easily accessible) kinds of experiences, I layer the six principles of embodied cognition into the discussion to show that spending time outdoors can exploit our innate preferences for learning. While each of us may not find it feasible to offer the full range of immersive nature experiences, as a collective, we can make going outside a more normal event in the course of a student's college experience.

IMMERSIONS IN THE WILDERNESS

At the top of the nature pyramid are experiences that happen least often but are most intensely immersive and lengthy in duration. They may require traveling greater distances from urban centers or familiar landscapes to counteract our brains' preferences for known and predictable environments that allow us to remain on mental autopilot. These kinds of events, then, confront the second principle of embodied cognition: our ever-moving bodies prize efficiency. In order to learn, we need to channel bodily energy into noticing attentively and resist the urge to follow established expectations based on experience; that's a lot easier when the experience is novel. Such immersive experiences generally require a visit to a wilderness, a special environment that bears the fewest traces of human cultivation and is least controlled by humans: a wild place. The payoff for taking the time and trouble to immerse ourselves in a wilderness can be significant, with restorative effects for individuals as well as for humankind. Reflecting on the potential of nature to overcome our most dangerous human proclivity to tribalism, E. O. Wilson sees a closer tie to nature as our salvation: "Evolution has equipped us with a terrible capacity for destruction, but also, a sublime one, for cooperation. We just have to decide which one we will honor. The key, I believe, is to reclaim our place in the natural world. We belong to nature. Save that, and we can certainly save ourselves" (Shining Red Productions 2015, 1:41:08–44). When proposing and advertising an immersive wilderness program for students, we should foreground personal, social, and ethical benefits—beyond the academic outcomes—for pursuing the experience.

When the natural environment is the primary object of your study, and you're taking students into an unfamiliar landscape and climate, the learning can be especially profound, as well as pleasurable. My Columbus State University colleagues, biologist Cliff Ruehl and geologist Clint Barineau (personal communication, 2018), report that "doing science," moving through the process of the scientific method while on site, allows the experience to instill and reinforce academic knowledge. Serendipity often allows students to witness a particular species or phenomenon that they can immediately place in the context of classroom learning, creating real-time excitement. Traveling to a wild environment requires both an openness to risk and an ability to settle in and absorb new ideas in the midst of unpredictable distractions. This adjustment to random and fleeting sensory stimuli, stochastic and ephemeral connections with nature, can take several days. Likewise, it takes time for a makeshift learning place—the boat, a van, a campsite—that might provoke an initial sense of disorientation to gradually become reclassified in students' minds as a classroom site.

There's a side benefit to the time it takes to travel to a wilderness site and then realign your senses to natural stimuli: all the while, the group can be engaged in building strong, personal connections, with you and with each other. A study conducted by my multi-award-winning physicist colleague Kimberly Shaw with her undergraduate student Chloe Chambers singled out these relationships as a key factor in student motivation to succeed in STEM fields: "Participants in this study praised current STEM professors

Fig. 2.1. Biology students identifying species of fish while snorkeling in Belize. (Photograph by Clifton Ruehl, May 2016. Used by permission.)

who made strong, personal connections with their students and created an encouraging classroom environment conducive to learning. From this study, many students within the geosciences fields in particular noted the bonds formed between students and professors as a result of extensive fieldwork outside the school" (Shaw and Chambers 2017). Faculty can become more than content experts in these situations, morphing into coaches, cheerleaders, and inspirational role models. While students are making vital connections between their hands-on observations and academic knowledge, faculty report that pushing the group outside of physical comfort zones often leads to students' greatest thrill. Overcoming physical obstacles, like hiking up a mountain or canoeing for two days straight, gives students "a huge sense of accomplishment. Their faces light up; some get tears," recalls Clint Barineau (personal communication, 2018). A strenuous physical experience builds confidence and character, leaving students with a transformed sense of their own capabilities. Some necessary pain and suffering can also mean that a feeling of reward is delayed, which my colleagues jokingly classify as "type 2 fun": not fun at the moment but quite satisfying to recall as a distant memory.

Research on the dopamine and pleasure responses of subjects shows strong results in environments where elements of risk or peril are present (see Terrapin 2014, 12). Would it seem wise to introduce elements of risk or peril in an academic program? Students afflicted with some degree of ecophobia are especially vulnerable, like Cliff Ruehl's student with arachnophobia, who spent several stuffy nights in the tropics fully zipped into her sleeping bag. When students threaten to become a liability to themselves and to the program's success, the coaching skills of a faculty member are especially critical. The recommendations of biophilic designers for introducing people to elements of risk or peril are to include measures of safety as we build confidence with higher-risk environments: make use of railings and viewpoints behind windows or observation from a greater distance. One study shows that writing about a phobia for as little as ten minutes can help the prefrontal cortex build strength to overcome the panic signals from fear centers in the brain (see Kircanski et al. 2012).

A growth mindset is essential for bringing students (and maybe ourselves) from a place of fear or aversion to the strong pleasure response that experiences in nature can provide. Human beings' range of tolerance is possible to expand as we contribute increasingly diverse events to our experience. Even genetic traits can be expressed or suppressed through factors external to the body, so that highly sensitive and delicate people can develop a hardier, more resilient response to risk—the orchid can become more like the dandelion, in John Ratey's (2014, 236) metaphor. My colleagues note that good food and hydration are especially critical in keeping up students' morale during challenging programs, testifying to the importance of continuously monitoring students' available bandwidth. And it's worth noting that perceptions of risk or peril are always relative, since program directors' experience levels are generally much higher and our perception of risk therefore lower than students' own.

But what if you're not a biologist or geologist or in a nature-related field of study? What can be done in academic fields that would seem disconnected from an intense nature-immersion experience? One key may be in looking for connections to a landscape that has been influential for a figure, culture, or mode of artistic expression your students take as an object of study. Place-based learning strategies make the most of embodied learning by bringing students' physical selves to a location they can inhabit and literally absorb through their senses, and these are sometimes remote locales. If you have the ability to design and lead a program that would involve travel away from your campus, consider spots that might bring together academic learning within a wilder landscape: the poetry, art, music, language, or philosophy of a region or figure who was shaped by an untamed natural environment; the economic, political, or historical events that have led to currently preserved wilderness space or threaten its continued existence. Institutions such as Prescott College in Arizona lead wilderness orientation camps for entering first-year students, which lend themselves to a nature-immersion experience as a means of developing increased self-awareness as well as academic preparation, through outdoor discussions and journaling. The Expedition Education Institute is designed for students to spend a gap year or semester recharging their enthusiasm for learning by living and learning outside. Students anywhere can be introduced to the idea that spending time in nature is an essential element to leading a healthy life. The opportunity to explore and discover the natural world in a wilderness can lead not only to creative insights about the object of your academic study but can be deeply restorative for both students and their program leaders.

Campus change-makers will want to consider equity in developing immersive programs for students; careful decisions about the program's length and a commitment to keeping expenses down will be important (and may necessitate seeking external program funding), as will be preparation to make participation accessible for all students. If you're game for developing an immersive program in a landscape and climate distant from your campus region, here are some summary recommendations to keep in mind:

- Pitch the program as an opportunity for personal and social growth, in addition to deep academic learning.
- Consider ways to build a positive sense of community en route to your destination, and during the trip.
- Give students time to adjust to natural stimuli; use mindfulness exercises to bring their awareness to the ways the new stimuli are acting on their bodily responses.
- Call attention to the dislocation of your learning space.
- Build safety nets for students who need to overcome resistance or a phobia.
- Be patient with students who may be experiencing type 2 fun, and keep in mind that it may take months or years for them to process the opportunity.

A DAY IN THE FOREST, A BOTANICAL GARDEN, AT A LAKE, OR ON THE BEACH

One level down from the peak of the nature pyramid is a recommended daylong outing to a place still largely removed from the sounds of traffic and manmade noise. Simply moving and thinking in a natural space addresses embodied cognition principle 1: like clouds or waves, our bodies are in a constant state of motion. As Florence Williams (2017, 166) notes from her meta-analysis of research and first-hand experience: "Nature appears to act directly upon our autonomic systems, calming us, but it also works indirectly, through facilitating social contact and through encouraging exercise and physical movement." By finding ways to take students outside for extended periods of time, we are supporting their overall well-being and thereby optimizing their abilities to learn. Studies from the past couple of decades support the critical necessity of physical activity for overall health (see Mandsager 2018). A recent Finnish study concludes that exercise while outdoors improves long-term well-being more than exercise indoors. "Good emotional well-being, in particular," state the authors, "seems to be evidently associated with more frequent, active visits to natural environments" (Pasanen et al. 2014, 340). Taking students on a nature field trip, then, requires more than bussing everyone to a forest or beach and then spending your time there sitting on benches. Your plan should involve activity: exploring some feature of the site in groups or with a planned topic for discussion.

Incorporating physical activity into your plan for a field trip offers a chance to model how critical exercise is to optimal brain functioning. The scientific evidence continues to mount in support of our cell-level dependence on aerobic exercise for brain growth and wellness. The discovery of brain-derived neurotrophic factor (BDNF) helped scientists account for the way exercise reliably enhances working memory, protecting existing neurons and promoting the growth of new ones, like a fertilizer for the brain. As cognitive scientist and Barnard College president Sian Beilock (2015, 185) summarizes, "Aerobic exercise is a catalyst for the appearance of metabolic nutrients necessary to think sharply. . . . Exercise helps grow new connections in the brain and strengthen existing ones; older adults who exercise have the brains of much younger people; young kids who are the most physically fit score the highest on important tests of achievement; and people who exercise regularly report worrying less and are less depressed than their sedentary counterparts." Students increasingly suffering from anxiety and depression stand much to gain from regular exercise. If the potential benefits aren't persuasive enough, the penalty for inactivity is also serious, amounting to brain impairment. Sedentary lifestyles are a preventable cause of chronic and fatal disease, estimated by the World Health Organization to cause two million premature deaths each year, a number that has increased exponentially each decade (see Lees and Booth 2004, 448). As health researchers argue, our increasingly sedentary habits should be classified as a public health epidemic. We're built to move. Physician and neuroscientist Daniel Wolpert (2011) argues that our large and complex brains may have developed to support our bodies' complex movements, which we've impressively recruited for other mental functions. These intellectual capacities, in order to develop and thrive, rely on biochemical processes naturally produced through physical exercise. We're doing our students and ourselves a favor to plan a vigorous outing in fresh air while spending extended learning time together.

The Association of Nature and Forest Therapy Guides and Programs offers a free online starter kit with eight steps to guide a two- to four-hour excursion with the explicit goal of improving health and well-being. Qing Li's *Forest Medicine* (2012) informs a growing school of *shinrin yoku* (forest therapy) practitioners, who lead guided walks through woodlands and offer instruction for accessing the deep relaxation that promotes better immune responses. Intriguing new studies suggest that specific kinds of olfactory stimulation produced by deep breathing in dense forests can improve the state of our immune systems (see Song et al. 2016). While a forest therapy session does involve movement and walking, its physical activity is gentle. Here's a brief description of the activity from the association's general guidelines:

- You won't go very far, often only a half mile or less. It's about being here, not getting there.
- Your primary goal is not to get a workout. It's more like playtime with a meditative feeling. If you find yourself working out, just pause for a moment of stillness, then proceed again slowly.
- While you can forest bathe in any natural environment, ideally your walks should take place in a wooded environment, with streams and meadows and minimal intrusion from human-made sounds such as traffic or construction.
- The trail should be accessible and easy to walk on. Go unplugged, without technological barriers between your senses and the forest. (Clifford 2018, 3)

While moving slowly, then finding one spot to sit or stand for twenty minutes or so, the major focus of forest therapy should be noticing. Close, deliberate observation of one's surroundings is combined with a careful awareness of bodily sensations and sensory stimuli, which leads to a calming feeling of connection with the earth. Whether your planned outdoor activity is a gentle forest bath or something more vigorous, improving students' overall health can help them to learn better in your class and in their other classes.

Forest bathing could be a tough sell for a department chair or dean to grant funds for a field trip. How can you tie academic outcomes directly to a daylong nature outing? One option may be to look for extensive grounds at a museum, performance venue, or historical site that you plan to visit for academic enrichment. Your visit to the exhibit or performance could incorporate an extended picnic lunch or outdoor break that explicitly engages students in exploring the grounds while placing into context the new information or impressions they're gaining. Another way to tie outdoor movement to academic learning is to follow in the (literal) steps of Bonnie Smith Whitehouse and Holly Huddleston, whose Belmont University creative writing and health and fitness concepts courses are cross-listed. Whitehouse's *Afoot and Lighthearted: A Journal for Mindful Walking* (2019) includes dozens of writing prompts to accompany reflective walks. As embodied cognition principle 6 reminds us, humans are infovores; our bodies reward us with pleasurable sensations for noticing new things and thereby acquiring new information. Taking a break from routine campus sights and sounds fosters the right conditions for this learning pleasure.

As soundscape studies have established, even ambient noise we become used to (passing car traffic, airline flight paths, landscaping or construction noise) can continue to cause startle responses in our systems, causing an allostatic load that leads to poor immune functioning. Humans have a distinct need for periodic silence and for natural sounds; we demonstrate a shared preference for the nature trifecta of wind, water, and birds, in particular: "Birdsong is stochastic, random and non-repeating, so our brains interpret it not as language but as a kind of background soundtrack. In fact, birdsong has some uncanny similarities to human-made music, and its range and technical wizardry might, on some unconscious level, stimulate our happy-music neurons" (Williams 2017, 98–99). As biophilic design research suggests, non-rhythmic sensory stimuli positively impact heart rate, systolic blood pressure, and sympathetic nervous system activity (see Terrapin 2014, 12). Other facets of a natural environment—natural light, air flow, the presence of water and plant life—can reduce stress, enhance cognitive performance, and positively impact mood. Encourage students to move, breathe, listen, and note their bodily responses. In order to call attention to these benefits, you can ask students to share their own experiences though short journal reflections or a comparison chart that draws from studies on biological responses to nature (fig. 2.2).

To maximize a daylong outing to any site connected to your disciplinary content, consider the following ideas:

- Look for natural sites like forests, gardens, lakes, or beaches that will offer space protected from human-made noise and air pollution. Scout out in advance accessible pathways that all students can navigate.
- Build physical activity into your itinerary, either vigorous or gentle, and let your students know why.
- Offer students a chance to reflect on their bodily responses to natural elements, possibly with a prompt that shares scientific evidence and allows them to compare their own experiences.

BIOPHILIC PATTERN (Adapted from Terrapin Bright Green, LLC. 2014.)	PREDICTED RESPONSE based on scientific research	YOUR EXPERIENCE compared with the predicted response
Visual Connection with Nature. A view to elements of nature, living systems and natural processes. What did you notice about the view?	Improved mental engagement/ attentiveness	
Non-Visual Connection with Nature. Auditory, haptic, olfactory, or gustatory stimuli that engender a deliberate and positive reference to nature, living systems or natural processes. What did you hear, sense, smell, or taste?	Positively impacted cognitive performance	
Non-Rhythmic Sensory Stimuli. Stochastic and ephemeral connections with nature that may be analyzed statistically but may not be predicted precisely. Did you notice any random sights, sounds, smells, etc.?	Observed and quantified behavioral measures of attention and exploration	
Thermal & Airflow Variability. Subtle changes in air temperature, relative humidity, airflow across the skin, and surface temperatures that mimic natural environments. Did the temperature and breeze affect you?	Positively impacted concentration	
Prospect. An unimpeded view over a distance, for surveillance and planning. Did you occupy a spot that offered an overlook?	Reduced boredom, irritation, fatigue	
Refuge. A place for withdrawal from environmental conditions or the main flow of activity, in which the individual is protected from behind and overhead. Did you occupy a spot that offered shelter?	Improved concentration, attention and perception of safety	

Fig. 2.2. Asking for students' feedback about their experiences of outdoor learning helps to provide transparency. (Biophilic chart adapted from Terrapin Bright Green, 2014, "14 Patterns of Biophilic Design: Improving Health and Well-Being in the Built Environment," https://www.terrapinbrightgreen.com /report/14-patterns/.)

EXCURSIONS TO PARKS OR WATERWAYS

Campuses of colleges and universities have built into their essential components not only buildings but grounds: the Latin word *campus* can be translated as "field." We are lucky to inherit green spaces, fountains, waterways, and fields that provide us with convenient access for outdoor learning. Campus planners have always known what a recent study of sixteen- to eighteen-year-old students has proven: "Study breaks in green spaces improved wellbeing and cognitive performance of adolescents. It also found that larger green spaces, either parks or forests, have stronger positive impacts on wellbeing and cognitive performance than small parks" (Wallner et al. 2018). Students may pass through green spaces daily but much more rarely inhabit them as places for learning. Outdoor environments are uncontrolled climates. There's unpredictable weather; there are potential interruptions from leaf blowers, lawn mowers, or building construction; there may not be comfortable places for everyone to sit; and bees, mosquitoes, or ants may want to join the conversation. But consider the assumptions that underlie this list of problems: we shouldn't be made uncomfortably cold or hot or wet, even for brief periods; we expect students to sit down, be quiet, and listen as the primary mode of learning; and we have to be able to hear clearly one person speaking, for some duration of time. But taking our classes outside should not mean lecturing al fresco. Like the fairly radical adjustments we should make to accommodate more movement in our classrooms to improve learning, taking our classes outside involves significant rethinking of our accustomed practices.

We know that mindful movement and play are two means of increasing openness and curiosity, and these may be easier to achieve outside. Neurochemical reward responses produced by novelty happen naturally in an outdoors environment. "Enquiry mode," as Guy Claxton (2015, 115) names it, can be triggered by "the presence of an opportunity to explore a pertinent or novel aspect of the current situation": "If a preliminary appraisal (by the body-brain) judges that the situation contains significant threats, fear or anger modes—fight or flight—might override enquiry (*as they often do in classrooms, for example*). But if things look interesting, safe, and relevant enough, then inquiry leads you to make an (appropriately cautious) approach and initiate investigation. . . . The happiness that follows learning we might call mastery or a satisfying sense of comprehending that which was previously obscure" (emphasis mine). Claxton's condition for the situation to be "interesting, safe, and relevant enough" offers a road map to designing an effective activity for outside learning. The trick is to connect a topic in your course content with a place you and your students can walk to and to use the space as a means for them to embody the knowledge.

"You Are There" reading experiences can be a powerful way of accessing embodied cognition principle 5: knowledge is embodied. In her book *Ex Libris*, Anne Fadiman (1998, 67) recounts memorable experiences in which she sets out to read important books in their original settings: "I have read Yeats in Sligo, Isak Dinesen in Kenya, and John Muir in the Sierras. By far my finest You-Are-There hour, however, was spent reading the journals of John Wesley Powell, the one-armed Civil War veteran who led the first expedition down the Colorado River, while I was camped at Granite Rapids in the bottom of the Grand Canyon." Fadiman describes reading Powell's narrative on the same banks of the roaring rapids he barely managed to survive and how thrilling it can be to cross the "eidetic threshold": a place of unusually vivid and detailed mental imagery supplied by reading, suddenly come to life in front of one's own eyes. Her experience testifies to the power of our senses in absorbing the recounted experiences of others.

Reading has the capacity to develop our insights into others' ways of thinking and feeling. First-person narratives in particular compel a reader to inhabit the consciousness of a fictional protagonist, a poem's speaker, or the mind of the memoirist. Historian Howard Zinn (2005, 193) has argued for greater use of literary texts like novels, poems, and memoirs in the teaching of history: "Students should learn the words of the people themselves, to feel their anger, their indignation. . . . These writings have an emotional impact that can't be found in an ordinary recitation of history." What connections might you make to the personal writing of scientists, artists, philosophers, political activists, teachers, inventors, or any important thinkers in your field? If it's possible to take students to a place that evokes the life or work of a key figure in your discipline, a powerful learning experience for students can be achieved by asking them to read the figure's own words aloud.

As part of a first-year writing course, I've taken students on a walking tour of our riverside city campus, to locations they themselves selected from passages in Carson McCullers's *The Heart Is a Lonely Hunter* (1940). The novel is set in a fictional town but clearly drawn from places in Columbus, Georgia, where McCullers was born and raised. Students stood in front of our courthouse and read aloud a dramatic scene in which Dr. Copeland, the novel's black physician, is arrested by the white sheriff; we proceeded several blocks along the route he was dragged to the old city jail, read further, and listened to a recording of the 1927 song

"Columbus Stockade Blues." Over a seventy-five-minute class period, we visited four or five locations and read the relevant passages on site. The students' willingness to finish this long novel was powerfully affected by our "You Are There" reading tour. Adding time for reflection or journaling outside allows students to capture new understandings or insights, as well as provides everyone with a healthy nature fix.

Think of the entire campus as a potential learning gallery: Which locations might lend themselves even indirectly to an embodied understanding of a concept from your course? What skills are you teaching that could be enhanced by going outside: describing, comparing, judging, valuing, creating? Some summary thoughts about taking your students out into the grounds of your campus:

- Where are your institution's fields, waterways, or grounds meant to provide natural refreshment?
- Can you create an interesting, safe, and relevant connection between any of these spots and your subject matter?
- How will you build activity into your outdoor exploration?
- How will you build in time for students to absorb a nature fix and to reflect on their learning?

DAILY ENVIRONMENTS

The lowest level of the nature pyramid involves everyday experiences that can be simple, rather fleeting, and not even necessarily outside: looking out windows, spending time with a pet, watering houseplants. But the natural environment can provide critical bandwidth recovery. Research has shown that exposure to green space has a disproportionately positive effect on the health of those in the lowest socioeconomic levels and mitigates social isolation (see Mitchell

2015; Cartwright et al. 2018). It may be especially critical to take our most vulnerable students outside. As his educational work with students of low socioeconomic status nationwide has convinced MacArthur Fellow Bill Strickland (2018) to conclude, "People are a function of environments." Can we blame students for a lack of intellectual curiosity when they sit and stare at projection screens in classrooms with the blinds pulled tightly shut? Embodied cognition principle 3 reminds us that our efficient bodies extend our cognitive capacities by harnessing our proximate surroundings, so we act in the best interest of learning by providing stimulating and health-promoting environments.

Biophilic design principles based on cognitive research (see Terrapin 2014) suggest that areas with a view ("prospect," in design parlance) improve comfort and perceived safety while reducing boredom, irritation, and fatigue. Sheltered areas (providing what designers call "refuge") can improve concentration and attention. The presence of natural light and fresh air can positively impact comfort, well-being, and productivity. Paying attention to the atmospheric conditions of your learning space matters for your students' success. Keep these principles in mind when searching for an outdoor spot the class can occupy for small group conversations.

Figure 2.3 illustrates nicely the principles of prospect and refuge. Students are working in small groups, which helps to mitigate potential difficulties with distraction. If you hold a traditional discussion (one voice at a time) outside, students will have more trouble maintaining focus in the midst of stochastic interruptions—for the same reasons it takes time for students to adjust to learning in the wilderness.

Recently, I held a traditional class discussion in a sheltered pavilion outside our assigned classroom building; we

Fig. 2.3. Choosing an outdoor spot that offers both a view and a sense of shelter is ideal; small group activities keep attention focused. (Photograph by Nick Norwood, 2018. Used by permission.)

sat at four tables with benches and looked out over both a sloping hill and people coming and going through the main entrance to the building. I created a Biophilic Experience Chart (fig. 2.2) to solicit my students' responses, which affirmed the research and also pointed to a flaw in my pedagogical strategy. Here is a selection of their anonymous comments, marked to highlight both **positive** responses and <u>negative</u> ones:

- "I think being outside helped me be **more awake** due to the lighting and temperature but also because it is not as quiet as indoors."
- "I do think there's something to be said for the **alertness** that being outside in the fresh air does compared to the sometimes stifling classroom."
- "The things that were going on around us forced us to stay more **alert** to avoid being <u>distracted</u>."

- "I tend to be <u>distracted</u> easily so the people walking by speaking loud took my attention. The construction also was <u>distracting</u>. But the birds and breeze **relaxed my mind** and helped with learning."
- "Being placed in a new environment has kept the lesson as a **unique memory**."

Students agreed that being outside was helpful for their **alertness** and made the discussion **relaxing and memorable**. But their heightened awareness (in other words, the thwarting of their predictive "autopilot" brains) made it hard for them to manage <u>distraction</u>. My plan should have included small group tasks, preferably that promoted movement, and keeping to a minimum the need for sustained attention on one person speaking. Embodied cognition principle 4 reminds us that other people affect our brains, both in positive and in negative ways. When we're going outside, we should plan activities designed to produce positive and productive social interactions among the group.

Daily interactions with nature might mean simply raising your classroom window blinds. A study by geographer Richard Ulrich (1984, 421) showed that hospital patients whose rooms permitted a window view to trees "had shorter postoperative hospital stays, had fewer negative evaluative comments from nurses, took fewer moderate and strong analgesic doses, and had slightly lower scores for minor postsurgical complications." Our students may not be recovering from surgery, but in classrooms they are physically institutionalized in a way not unlike people who are sick or imprisoned (!), so we should at least let them look out the window. Moving outside sends a meaningful, concrete signal to counteract this comparison. And as I mentioned in the previous chapter, we could stand to take a few lessons from our progressive colleagues in preschool education. Acting on the best-selling work of Richard Louv, *Last Child in the Woods* (2005), hundreds of preschool educators have established nature-based preschools, in which children spend all or part of the day outside. One such school takes place at the University of Washington's Botanic Gardens; the students explore the arboretum in poor weather. Other schools have no indoor facility at all.

Regional climates dictate what sort of investments are necessary for outdoor learning, as experts acknowledge: "One of the big things we say in the nature-based-education world is there's no such thing as bad weather, only poor choices in clothing" (Madison Powell, quoted in Depenbrock 2017). Owning appropriate clothing to go outdoors in any kind of weather raises a potential cost barrier. If we want to get serious about improving students' well-being and therefore their learning, we need to be upfront about a potential shift in resources required by individuals and by the institution. How many slideshow projector bulbs might equal the cost of an outdoor clothing bank for students, more shade trees, or well-maintained, accessible pathways?

. . . .

Part Two

LEVERAGE THE BODY FOR LEARNING

Chapter Three

. . . .

INTERROGATE SENSORY PERCEPTIONS

. . . .

The science behind sensory-enhanced, movement-based learning activities shows why they work: bodies play an indispensable role in cognitive processes. If our brains are generally on autopilot as a way to conserve energy, learning new ideas demands energy that must be summoned from our bodies. The state of our immune systems, our levels of hormones, our relative amounts of rest and nutrition, all affect the amount of energy we can summon to actively test sensory input against predictions from known experience. As Lisa Feldman Barrett (2017a, 65) explains, when either sensory input or prediction errors are being ignored, we are not learning, although we do enter other states: a state of daydreaming or imagination relies on predictions and shuts out sensory input, while a meditative state observes sensory input detached from predictive judgment.

The energy-intensiveness of learning helps to explain the vividness of childhood experiences, during which we are forming the neural pathways that will inform future predictions. Our feeling that time passes more quickly as we grow older can be understood as a reflection of brain efficiency: the once-thrilling excitement of blowing out candles on a cake becomes quickly processed as "birthday," *check*. Nothing new to see here, says the predictive brain; move right along. That comfortable and low-energy state is exactly what we need to shake up in a classroom full of adults, including young adults. Infusing classroom activities with embodied, sensory experiences may confirm our intuition that fun activities can enhance learning but also risks eliciting scorn from colleagues (and students) who perceive as "childish" anything aside from sitting still and paying attention. The legacy of our long history of industrial-age education will be slow to shed: "Just as Victorian factory workers were taught to be docile employees, the baton their educational system handed to us is that we in the 21st century are teaching our children to be sedentary. Our schooling is imparting to them that sitting for long periods is normal and something to be prepared for in adult life" (Cregan-Reid 2018a, 197). By offering sensory-rich experiences, we offer a more compelling invitation to revise learners' known experiences. Complicating the picture is the fact that we can't trust our brains to process sensory input objectively; the ecosystem of the body and brain always affects our perceptions.

In his book *Behave* (2017), neuroendocrinologist Robert Sapolsky considers the implications of recent research studies probing body/mind integration. Using functional magnetic resonance imaging (fMRI) technology, neuroscience is now seeking empirical evidence for territory explored in the past by language philosophers. Conceptual metaphors may be literally evoked by physical sensations: job interview candidates were considered "weightier" by some study participants when their résumés were attached to a heavier clipboard. Strangers' personalities were judged to be more "warm" or "cold" if the perceivers were holding hot or cold beverages. Our judgments may be altered by sitting in hard or soft chairs and by whether or not we've recently eaten or feel hungry. Our inclination to confuse moral guilt with the need for a shower has been labeled as the Macbeth (or Pontius Pilate) Effect; in some of these experiments, subjects selected gift samples of mouthwash after fibbing and hand sanitizer after composing lies in writing. Neuroimaging showed that the parts of the brain associated with the mouth or the hand were activated during the experiment, potentially suggesting that the body/mind connection is not just a general phenomenon but can be quite specific to parts of the body. Although undeniably fascinating, the replicability of the Macbeth Effect has been problematic (see Earp et al. 2014). Sapolsky (2017, 568) asks as he surveys the research, "What's going on in these studies? Metaphors about weight, density, texture, temperature, interoceptive sensations, time, and distance are just figures of speech. Yet the brain confusedly processes them with some of the same circuits that deal with the physical properties of objects." Sapolsky accounts for this fascinating predilection of our minds by referring to scientific research on "neural reuse" (Anderson 2014; Lakoff 2012). These studies suggest that our evolving brains are improvising, mapping more recently evolved abstract conceptual (especially moral) thinking onto well-established neural pathways designed for sensory input. So while we're offering sensory-rich experiences, we must remain vigilant about our own mental processing of them. Thinking critically about how our own brains are working might be the most valuable form of critical thinking we can teach. If we can achieve some detachment from our own perceptions, we are less susceptible to instinctive or rigid behaviors that may not be serving us well.

AFFECTIVE REALISM AND NOTICING

Human thinking is structured through our experiences in the physical world, and linguistic evidence reveals this embodied understanding. Cognitive linguist Mark Johnson (1987, 108 and 7) has studied how our bodily experiences within a physical environment shape our ways of speaking. A simple example of his evidence includes *understanding as seeing*: we express understanding as "getting the picture," "illuminating," or having a "point of view." Another example is *bodily appearance as a physical force*: an appealing person is described as a "knockout," "devastating," "striking," a "bombshell," "radiant," or "attractive," so that one is "blown away" or "melts." Johnson demonstrates how a whole range of image schemata pervades human imagination, allowing us to make sense of our thoughts and feelings through references to bodily experience. To cite a historical example, consider the piercing, painful sensation of forbidden or unrequited romantic love, expressed by poets through the classical figure of Cupid, who shoots lovers through the heart or eyes with his sharp arrows. As Barrett (2017a, 79) expounds, "You might think that in everyday life, the things you see and hear influence what you feel, but it's mostly the other way around: that what you feel alters your sight and hearing. Interoception [your sense of your internal state] in the moment is more influential to perception, and how you act, than the outside world is." Let's pause to consider that paradox: we know that our senses are irrevocably bound up in our cognitive processing of an event, but our internal processes are at the same time shaping our sensory perceptions. This phenomenon testifies to the amazingly porous boundary between the mental and the physical.

Not only do our thoughts and feelings influence our sensory perceptions, they can actually delude us into believing that we have seen, heard, smelled, or even eaten things that we simply imagined. This happens because of the second principle of embodied cognition: our brains prefer to conserve energy by predicting what should be happening, based on past experience or on absorbed images (say, from entertainment or news media) or on information we've been primed to accept. When a witness to a crime testifies that the assailant was carrying a gun, that sensory "knowledge" is more likely to have come from predictions based on expectations of the witness's brain than on actual conditions—especially if the witness's brain was trying to conserve energy in anticipation of a fight-or-flight moment. In an experiment with taste testers of milkshakes, cognitive psychologist Alia Crum showed that actual levels of the hunger-signaling peptide ghrelin measured in subjects' bloodstreams differed by significant amounts depending upon whether subjects thought they had consumed calorie-rich "Indulgence" shakes or low-fat "Sensi-shakes," though the two shakes were exactly the same. Crum's research on the placebo effect affirms the science of embodied cognition by providing evidence that our bodies sense what our brains predict to be true (Stanford SPARQ 2018).

Understanding the way the body is involved in making meaning has a number of important implications for teaching and learning practice. First, it should underscore how inextricable and intertwined are our physical environment, sensory perception, and cognitive understanding. Second, and more complicated, it means that even as we can leverage the environment and the senses to deepen learning, we must be on guard against affective realism, or the ways that our internal conditions shape our perception of an external world. The brain's instinct to conserve energy by relying on prediction means that confronting new and unfamiliar input demands real energy from our systems. If our bodies are already low in energy or perceive that we need to economize in anticipation of future demand, we are a lot less willing to expend energy on the priority of testing and revising our brains' predictions. "In a sense," writes Barrett (2017a, 65), "your brain is wired for delusion." Understanding that our brains are vulnerable to evolutionary adaptations that inform our perceptions and judgments can help us to be on guard against our own instincts or intuitions while developing more deliberate habits of mind.

The framework of Object-Based Learning (OBL), practiced most widely by anthropologists, art historians, museum educators, and those whose fields of study focus on material objects, offers a useful means of guiding students through multisensory learning. OBL strategies ask students to slow down and make careful, deliberate observations of their perceptions of objects, which leverages the senses while acknowledging their tricky relationship with the brain. Knowledge is constructed through embodied experience, as we know from principle 5, and that process starts when we slow down to carefully observe, to notice. Two points may be useful to keep in mind. First, sensory activities, especially those like smell and touch less expected in the classroom, help to develop skills in noticing. Second, sensory activities should facilitate an awareness of how our senses interact with feelings and perception, enhancing or possibly misconstruing reality. Some educational theorists have drawn a distinction between the senses of sight, hearing, and touch (so-called "cognitive senses" because they can provide our brains with information about form, structure, and category) and the senses of smell and taste, which are considered to offer "qualitative" information that engages the emotions (Zull 2011, 49). Yet embodied cognition research indicates that such distinctions are not so clear-cut. Because all of our sensory input is subject to interoceptive networks and the brain's predictive behaviors, any of the senses can offer meaningful ways to engage deeper learning as well as to think critically about perception. Acknowledging the complex nature of sensory perception can usefully promote an inclusive learning environment; every human has shifting degrees of sensitivity and sensory limitation that make us vulnerable in various contexts and stronger when we leverage group diversity. Using a variety of sensory learning activities can provide a range of alternatives for all students. For the sake of organizational simplicity, the examples that follow focus on each sense, one at a time, in terms of the specific learning goals they can help to facilitate. Activities that make use of multiple senses, however, offer the most powerful learning experiences.

SIGHT: RETHINKING VISION

Object-Based Learning coaches students to develop special observational skills to describe, classify, and analyze. What objects does your discipline value: artifacts? rocks? bones? visual art? maps? books? Jessica Metzler of Brown University's Sheridan Center for Teaching and Learning guides learners through close-looking exercises as a scaffold for further research and inquiry. As she demonstrated in a 2018 "Ways of Seeing" pre-conference workshop for the Professional and Organizational Development Network, Metzler moves from "what?" to "so what?" to "now what?" as learners look closely and then raise questions that emerge organically. Below are the steps in an OBL process from her workshop:

- What? Ask students to spend ten minutes or longer looking closely at an unfamiliar object and making notes about what they see. Share with the class or small group the details that emerge. Next, make a series of two-minute drawings of the object: try to outline its shape without looking down at the page; attempt to shade in the "negative space" around the object; select and sketch one detail of the object. The point is not to produce excellent sketches, but to exercise observational skills.

- So what? Lead a "carousel" round of inquiry by giving students two minutes to write their initial questions about the object they've been observing at the top of a page, then pass the page to another person for a two-minute extension and addition of questions, and again for a third round. Have students work in small groups to sort the assembled questions into themes or categories.

- Now what? Ask students to formulate ideas about how and where they might begin to answer the questions that have been raised. As you share a "big reveal" moment to share what is known by experts about the object, the sources of expert information and stories of how it has been established can provide context for students' own further research work.

As they begin to look closely and notice details, students will need to learn and practice the appropriate disciplinary vocabulary. Once won't be enough; seeing something new and articulating it through newly acquired terminology takes lots of repetition, immediate feedback to reinforce, and spaced opportunities for retrieval.

Since we know from the first principle of embodied cognition that our bodies are in constant motion, it makes sense to combine looking with moving around the learning space. In *Student Engagement Techniques*, Elizabeth F. Barkley (2010,

170) describes one in-class strategy called "Stations": "It engages students by requiring them to move around the room [or building, or beyond] and interact with learning materials in an active way as they examine, question, exchange ideas with peers, respond to prompts, and formulate their own thoughts and commentary. Exhibits can be simple (flip chart paper with a question written on it) or elaborate (an interactive multi-sensory presentation)." The gallery objects should encourage students to view objects critically, formulating possible solutions to a problem or collecting data for interpretations. "Stations" also lends itself to getting outside and might ask students to discover specific kinds of objects in a scavenger hunt. Creating a gallery exercise taps into principle 6 of embodied cognition, our bodies reward learning, because providing incomplete or partial information to be completed by noticing stimulates curiosity and our desire to close the information gap.

In the case of sight, we have an opportunity to help students interrogate vision as a source of unfiltered reality, or the belief that our senses provide us with reliable, objective perceptions. The brain interprets signals sent by our eyes, but exactly what we perceive can be complex, broken down into separate systems for processing different aspects such as imagery, motion, form, color, texture, and function (Ramachandran 1998, 66–72). Differences in focus can lead some people to describe an underwater ocean photograph as populated by a colorful variety of creatures, and others, in the same image, by a single menacing shark. The phenomenon of *inattentional blindness*, most famously demonstrated by the "invisible gorilla" experiment by Christopher Chabris and Daniel Simons (2012), illustrates the powerful influence of our minds on our sense of sight: "In our best-known demonstration, we showed people a video and asked them to count how many times three basketball players wearing white shirts passed a ball. After about 30 seconds, a woman in a gorilla suit sauntered into the scene, faced the camera, thumped her chest and walked away. Half the viewers missed her. In fact, some people looked right at the gorilla and did not see it." Inattentional blindness makes us miss a lot of things while we're primed to notice others. When verbal cues are provided, even objects that are obscured by scribbles or blurry boundaries become suddenly visible (see Lupyan and Ward 2013). Research on aesthetics has identified particular patterns as having innate visual appeal for humans, so that we are biased to prefer geometric fractal images produced by nature—brilliantly employed by contemporary artists like Piet Mondrian and Jackson Pollack (see Taylor 2002; Spehar 2003). It should come as no surprise that humans also like landscape paintings that feature prospect and refuge: wide views from a safe perspective.

Our energy-conscious brains mostly see what we are expecting to see, sometimes even leading us to see what is not there. Using optical illusions to illustrate our own mental vulnerabilities offer a valuable lesson in remaining critical of our perceptions, both concrete and abstract. Neurologist V. S. Ramachandran uses an image of shaded circles to reveal our brains' visual assumptions as deeply informed by our embodied experience. The circles are all identical but shaded either on the top or on the bottom halves. We see the circles as convex that are lighter on the top, and as concave that are darker on the top (to see an image of this illusion, search online for "dimples or bumps"). "This is because," Ramachandran (1998, 69) explains, "the visual areas in your brain have a built-in sense that the sun is shining from above." The coloring of some animals exploits this phenomenon to attract mates (think peacock feathers) or to look less appealing as prey (think gazelles) (see Ramachandran 2008). In lectures for her Yale-cum-Coursera course, "The Science of Well-Being," positive psychologist Laurie Santos uses a series of optical illusions to illustrate our brains' tendencies toward "miswanting" or seeking happiness from the wrong sources. The first and most basic illusion, two equal lines made to appear different lengths by directional arrows pointing in on the ends of one line and pointing out on the ends of the other, allows her to show that our minds' strongest intuitions are often wrong. Even when we measure the lines and prove to ourselves that they're equal, our eyes can't stop perceiving them as different. The fallacy doesn't disappear even when we know how it works. That illusion provides a concrete example of why knowing facts isn't always enough to change our perceptions.

SOUND: INTENSIFYING IMPACT

In the same way that OBL develops students' skills for close observation, listening exercises can help students to focus their attention through sound. Our sense of hearing, especially hearing the sounds made by other human bodies, has been developed so acutely that we can detect "the mood, gender, socio-hierarchical status, or even some personality traits of [a] walking person by only listening to the footsteps in a hallway," as a Finnish study recaps recent research (see Saarela and Hari 2008). Cognitive scientists have investigated how we gather social information like group dynamics from the sounds of people walking in groups. Our auditory skills can be sharpened and interrogated through exercises that build observational skill, powers of description, and awareness of the ways social cues are communicated through a soundscape. Sound designers recommend beginning to develop students' sensitivity to a soundscape through a sound walk: "Sound walks were originally proposed by Murray Schafer [in *The Tuning of the World* (1977)] as an empirical methodology to identify and describe a soundscape of a specific location. When performing a sound walk, people are asked to navigate in a delimited area with open ears, remembering all the sounds heard. We ask students to perform such exercises in pairs, where one person is blindfolded and the other one acts as the guide" (Rocchesso et al. 2013, 128–29). The sound walk concludes with sharing among participants all of the sounds noted on the walk. In addition to calling attention to many ambient sounds to which we might become more sensitive, a reflective discussion could result in identifying sounds that were interpreted differently by students. What expectations govern what we think we are hearing?

Immersive listening can also function as a way to notice the wide range of information we gather through sound. *The Revenge*, an experimental play written for BBC radio by Andrew Sachs in 1978, is a thriller told strictly through sound effects, without any words at all. Using this twenty-four-minute play as a listening assignment with students poses a challenge to our assumptions about the role of language in making meaning. You might ask students to translate the story in words or in pictures; a post-listening discussion might ask them which sounds are most (and least) open to interpretation: Are the sounds made by human bodies (breathing, whistling) easier for us to decode than sounds made by inanimate objects? Do some sounds elicit embodied responses (raised heart rate or breathing, clenched fingers or toes, tense stomachs) from us as listeners?

Once students have developed some basic awareness of a soundscape, create your own immersive listening assignment with a relevant disciplinary text that tells a story—fictional, historical, or even a case study or important experiment. Read aloud or record yourself reading a primary source document or dense narrative text, slowly and with special attention to descriptive words. Ask students to listen intently as they close their eyes and imagine themselves in the scene being described; they might be themselves just observing the action, or they might put themselves in the place of someone identified in the text itself. On a second reading, provide a list of questions to have students move carefully through an imaginative exploration of their senses as they are listening to the narrative: What might they see as they look around? What could they hear in this place, nearby and farther away? How would the temperature of the air feel, and how would it smell? What might give off scents around them? How might the clothes that they are wearing feel on their skin? What might they be eating or drinking in this place, or (conversely) might they be quite hungry or thirsty at this moment? Encourage students to explore the impact of the exercise on their understanding of the narrative in a post-listening journal assignment.

Most of us are well aware of the way that listening to music or podcasts can entertain us by occupying our thoughts while our bodies are busy with routine tasks that don't require continuous monitoring: walking or running, long-distance driving, house cleaning, or yardwork. Neuroscience shows that our brains are actually wired to learn while we're physically moving: as José Antonio Bowen and C. Edward Watson (2017, 101) remind faculty, "You may have been good at learning while sitting still, but that is unusual." This is an opportunity to make use of the wide variety of podcasts (which are exploding in number and variety and often free) by creating or curating materials relevant to your subject that students can access through an audio app or player: lectures, interviews, works of fiction, or music. Encourage students to listen to the assigned material while dealing with an otherwise routine manual task that will not require much conscious attention—not other homework. Provide a few questions about key elements to focus their listening. Have them respond in writing immediately afterward to capture insights about the material. Ask students to share a metacognitive reflection about the assignment: how did routine physical activity affect the learning experience?

Finally, the importance of silence is worth noting: we spend our days enveloped in sound, whether through our own devices or the ambient noise of modern life, so achieving a state of silence often requires deliberate intention. Contemplative practitioner Patricia Owen-Smith (2018, 32) cautions that "research on silence and learning is still in its infancy," yet studies have shown that silence produces brain activity corresponding to increased states of insight and clarity. We can practice a purposeful silence in the classroom to call attention to our relative lack of it in modern life and for important shifts in our mental landscape at specific moments: for a few minutes at the beginning of class to let go of distractions, as intermittent pauses to absorb new ideas and material, or during a closing reflection exercise that could involve writing.

SMELL: LEVERAGING ATTENTION

Just as our perceptions of sights and sounds are context dependent, smell is hugely influenced by expectations. As embodied cognition principle 4 reminds us, each of us affects the embodied ecosystem of others, and we are acutely sensitive to social cues in interpreting smells. "The commonly acknowledged power of scent," explains psychologist and smell scientist Avery Gilbert (2008, 89), "derives in large part from the power of suggestion." Gilbert cites studies going back as far as 1899 in which people report strong sensations, even illness, based purely on being told that they were being exposed to a harmful odor. Aromatherapy can produce real benefits, but largely on the basis of specific, positive expectations. Our sense of smell is also remarkably ephemeral; we adapt to scents, making them harder to detect, and recover our sensitivity to a smell once we're away from the source. The intensity and specificity of smells affect our adaptive responses, so that we adapt more quickly to stronger odors but remain sensitive to other smells even in the presence of one overpowering aroma.

Gilbert's survey of scientific research on smell debunks the long- and widely held belief that this sense is uniquely connected to memory. Ever since Proust made popular the idea that the smell of a favorite pastry could instantly transport one into the past, scientists have been chasing evidence for this belief in the special association of smell and memory, without much success.

Why does it feel so magical when a sniff triggers a twinge of remembrance? A lot of it has to do with surprise. You weren't trying to remember the paints, oils, and solvents in Grandpa's workshop—the memory popped up, unasked for, when you walked through a random odor plume. Even more surprising: you never made a deliberate effort to memorize those smells when you were seven years old. If you had, the recollection would be no surprise. . . . The sense of wonder that comes with the experience is, like all magic, an illusion based on misdirection. Like a nightclub mentalist, the mind presents us with a memory it picked from our pocket when we weren't looking. (Gilbert 2008, 200–201)

Smells are more reliably remembered, argues Gilbert, when they're deliberately described and consciously evoked by concrete objects. In this respect, smell has classroom value that, while not exactly magical, can be useful for all of the same skill development as other senses: close observation and novelty as a means to pleasure in learning. Perhaps even better than sight and sound, smell can be leveraged to show how susceptible our senses are to contextual factors in perception.

Your lab or studio may inherently involve material with distinctive smells; do you call attention to these aspects of learners' experience? Taking time to allow students to describe carefully what they are smelling helps them to own and absorb the experience. If your subject doesn't involve distinctive-smelling material, consider bringing to class something to smell related to your topic. The scent could be indirectly connected (for example, the library's musty copy of a book by a relevant figure or a scent-rich item from a relevant place), but giving students time to smell the object and put into their own words its distinctive aroma will provide an additional way to experience and to literally internalize the material. As students put into their own words how the object smells to them, be attentive to how their feelings and expectations about the material may also shape their descriptions of its smell.

Smells are especially dependent on social cues. When one study primed subjects with food aromas (chocolate) connected to their identity as members of a cultural group (Swiss nationals), they smelled the associated aromas more favorably and intensely—and were more disgusted by smells associated with an out-group (Coppin et al. 2016). Even social aspirations to join an in-group can positively influence our perception of associated sensory cues. Can we leverage this in the classroom? How do students describe the smell of your lab or studio or classroom, your library, your campus? See if you can collaboratively identify the mix of sources that produce this unique smell and encourage class members to connect themselves with the students who have experienced the smell of this space in the past. How are you all members of a unique and valuable community?

Associations with smell can also be intentionally re-framed: could even an unlikely study environment (a fast-food kitchen, a city bus, a hospital waiting room) become reclassified in our minds as productive space? We can transform our perception of smells to work in our favor, even when we can't control the environment. Perhaps we need to recognize our negative response to certain smells as a rejection of people we regard as "them," not "us." We could choose to embrace spaces and their smells as part of our connection to a larger shared identity—those working hard to support ourselves or improve our lives, for example. Challenge students to create or recognize an effective study environment by paying attention to smell. What olfactory cues can students self-select as helping to eliminate distraction, to feel calm, or to induce sleep? Ask students to keep a log or journal of their study time, including what their most-used study spaces smell like. Does lighting a scented candle, opening up a window, or simply reframing the context make a difference? One study on memory consolidation found a significant improvement in subjects' retention of visual-spatial memory (the location of pieces in a puzzle) by memorizing in the presence of a scent that was reintroduced during deep sleep (Rasch et al. 2007). While the researchers found the results encouraging as a method of improving certain kinds of memory without an invasive or sleep-disturbing mechanism, the trick didn't work for other kinds of memory tasks, and the scent had to be reintroduced (by someone other than the sleeper!) at just the right stage of deep sleep. Smell scientist Gilbert might point out that this experiment mostly confirms the importance of sleep, not smell, in memory consolidation.

While smell isn't inherently more valuable for learning than other senses, its ability to deepen learning through sensory cues can work by introducing novelty. You might introduce smell as part of an icebreaker exercise at the beginning of the term. This activity treats scent as an affordance, or a way for us to engage a tool to extend our capacities, as recommended by embodied cognition principle 3. Ask students to choose a favorite scent to bring along to class—an orange peel, a candle, cut grass in an envelope, a clothes dryer sheet, or anything (legal!) they enjoy and consider distinctive. In circle groups of eight or fewer, have students take turns passing around each person's scent, repeating the associated person's name. At the end of the class or at the next session, have students test each other by using the scent only as a cue.

TASTE: CREATING COMMUNITY

Taste is intimately connected with smell and can be used in similar ways to enhance learning activities. The act of eating, moreover, adds a significant element of social connection and community. We know that each of us affects the embodied ecosystem of others from embodied cognition principle 4, and sharing a meal together is one of the most fundamental ways that human beings express trust and generosity. As a species, humans have particularly delicate digestive systems that developed to accommodate our upright postures and needs for mobility. As foragers, we can eat a wide range of things, but we pay the consequences for poor choices. The power of food and drink has the capacity for great positivity and can also pose psychological threat; the wide range of eating disorders, addictions, and biological intolerances testifies to our complex relationship with food. That tension makes incorporating taste a risky exercise in the classroom, but one that can result in outsized benefits.

Nutritional health plays a major role in cognitive performance, and we need to serve as institutional advocates for a deliberately supportive food culture on campus. The poor or irregular eating habits of most college students means that nutritional deficiency presents a real obstacle to learning. Supplying food as part of a special or difficult class activity builds community and offers literal sustenance for hungry students. While doughnuts, chips, and soda are easy to transport and make up a familiar college repertoire, think carefully about your options for providing food for bandwidth recovery. Consider alternatives: trail mix with nuts and dried fruit, cut vegetables with yogurt dip, dark chocolate bites, hard cheeses with whole grain crackers. You might even provide water at an early morning class; most people are slightly dehydrated then and will function better with some water (Bowen and Watson 2017, xvi). Your food choices can reflect an awareness of the role bodily health plays in facilitating learning. Students may not know much about nutrition or may find good food hard to afford or locate. This personal challenge can offer a valuable connection with your course subject matter. Hunger, including malnutrition, is a complex social, economic, and cultural topic relevant in a range of disciplines.

Because taste, like all senses, is affected by social and emotional context, our perception of how good something tastes can change depending on how connected we feel to a food's cultural identity. As a recent study using regional cuisines explains it, "preferences depend on the social identity contexts in which they are embedded—taking into account a person's long-term degree of social identification and the salience of a particular social identity in a given moment" (Hackel et al. 2018, 271–72). If your course includes learning about cultural groups within or outside of your home region, consider opportunities to bring samples of food or drinks authentic to the culture to share in class to help students connect their own identities (even temporarily, as students in your course) to the region of study. Field trips offer invaluable chances to broaden students' taste experiences: for inexpensive, nutritious, and culturally diverse options, consider a farmers' market for lunch. Unfamiliar tastes, like unfamiliar ideas, demand real bodily energy to process, which also offers an opportunity for students to examine their expectations about tasting something new. "Social identity may also lead people to evaluate out-group foods more negatively," as the regional cuisine study found, for instance, "feeling disgust toward the appearance, smell, or (as assessed in the current research) taste of out-group foods. These visceral experiences may promote or maintain negative attitudes toward an out-group" (Hackel et al. 2018, 278). To overcome implicit negative evaluations, researchers suggest appealing to a "superordinate" identity, or connection that reaches beyond an us-them divide. Can membership in your class, or as majors in your discipline, become a superordinate identity for your students? If it seems possible to cultivate a shared identity (maybe even as aspiring professionals or college-educated citizens), it may change students' willingness to try culturally unfamiliar food or drinks.

Finally, consider the role of taste in building relationships with students in your own office or in another common space on campus. Invite students to share a cup of tea or coffee as a preliminary gesture to facilitate important conversations. Knowing that you are a human being who eats and drinks can make a real difference for certain students who may find you less than approachable. Scheduling meetings with small groups of students (project teams, for instance) at a campus café can allow you to build relationships with and among them because of the basic trust expressed in sharing something to drink or eat.

TOUCH: EMBODYING CONCEPTS

"Skin is at once our most basic and most sophisticated organ, and touch is our prototypical sense," argues Guy Claxton (2015, 57), who considers other senses "merely specialized forms of touch." Like vision's dependence on locomotion for development, touch is also deeply integrated with movement, specifically manipulation, as haptic ("perception by touch") research shows: "Touch and movement are good examples of convergence of information between sensory modalities. In fact, without movement, the touched object cannot be clearly processed" (Ittyerah 2013, 113). We can use touch as a strategy for all three basic steps in embodied learning: noticing, imitating, and practicing. Touch offers us the chance to exploit our brains' evolutionary improvisation skills, or neural reuse. Because haptic sensations allow us to access conceptual thinking, we can harness that power for learning. As art educator Cheung On Tam (2015, 117) explains, an object that can be touched "becomes a vehicle for motivation, and one that encourages critical observation, formulates learning tasks and develops active enquiry."

Objects we can touch are especially appealing as affordances that allow our efficient bodies to make use of tools to extend our capacities, as we know from embodied cognition principle 3.

Multiple studies have shown that notetaking by hand rather than on a keyboard has cognitive benefits like better memory recall, conceptual development, and creativity (see Henry 2016). Notetaking in general, however, is highly dependent on students' clear understanding of what information they'll be asked to recall, and then practicing effective strategies for retrieving that information. Portable whiteboards or giant sticky notes with colored markers offer encouragement to record ideas and work creatively and collaboratively. Cognitive mapping offers students a chance to sketch out their understanding of the relationships among ideas in a nonlinear way. Giving students time to get up and move around to record individual or group ideas on whiteboards not only lessens personal risk but results in a space they've physically transformed with their own collective work. You might snap digital images of especially productive wall-work to post on your course learning management system or website.

Beyond using a writing tool to offload our thoughts onto a writing surface, we can use touch similarly to other sensory input to sharpen our observational skills. Anthropologist Andrew Causey (2015) offers several exercises that help with noticing and drawing mindful attention to the functions of ordinary objects from modern life. Like the sketching exercise mentioned in the vision section of this chapter, Causey recommends a drawing activity that involves placing an object inside of a paper bag, and asking students to create an outline of the object based purely on tactile exploration, feeling the object inside of the bag without being able to see it. A second exercise could work well as an icebreaker; "The Object Possessed" asks students to consider what their keychains reveal about their identities. Touching the keys and all other elements involved (its holder, rings, or lanyard), students are asked to share which parts of the keychain are most important, least important, most meaningful, and best represent their social identity (Causey 2015, 136–37).

Asking students to imitate an understanding of complex concepts can produce helpful insights about salient aspects of the topic. Chemistry educators have exploited touch as a learning tool for students to build models of three-dimensional molecules. First developed as a way for blind students to grasp concepts in chemistry, these strategies benefit all learners as an opportunity to imitate structures that are normally presented in a two-dimensional visual format. My colleagues Rajeev Dabke and Zewdu Gebeyehu (2010) have made use of common objects—paper clips, magnets, and ball bearings—as well as Lego sets to provide students with opportunities to build the periodic table and molecular shapes. By building physical models with materials that can correspond to the topic, students can make use of their own bodies as raw material. An exercise from the dance practice known as contact improvisation asks groups to form collective shapes with their bodies that imitate objects and experiences, then concepts; participants must construct the shapes without speaking to each other and under a tight time constraint. So a beginning challenge might be for groups to collectively represent concrete objects like a house or an experience like a car ride and eventually to find ways of imitating concepts like unity or civil rights.

Finally, using touch in the classroom facilitates practicing because physical structures can provide embodied metaphors for conceptual thinking. Another of the many relevant activities included in Elizabeth Barkley's *Student Engagement Techniques* (2010) provides exactly this connection between the concrete and the abstract. During a brainstorming exercise or to ignite discussion, for example, a "snowball" exercise begins with asking students to jot answers to a prompt on paper. Rather than asking for volunteers to share their own responses, students crumple up the pages and throw them around the room, picking up and tossing others' "snowballs" so that a fair amount of exchange takes place. Students can then be called at random to smooth out the papers and share the ideas they find. Barkley (2010, 145) notes this technique "works well to get lots of ideas out on the floor (literally!) and is a fun and energizing way to break up long stretches of class time." Special education and counseling professor Leila Ansari Ricci uses this activity to allow students to share more personal, narrative responses safely: "Because of the anonymity of this activity, the shared stories are potent, authentic, and often heart tugging" (Berrett and Supiano 2019). The strategy connects a physical act with a metaphorical meaning—getting ideas out on the floor—which can lessen the risk for students to contribute an unorthodox idea.

An exercise from Barkley, Major, and Cross's *Collaborative Learning Techniques* (2014) called "Trust Me!" offers students an experience of tangible interconnection before launching a collaborative assignment. Students create a physical web to build a conceptual metaphor for interdependence. The instructions for activity include suggested concrete-abstract correspondences:

> Arrange students in a circle and give one student a large ball of twine. This student begins by stating, "Group work is good for ____" (completing the sentence stem with a positive attribute

of group work). She then tosses the ball of string to the other side of the circle, hanging onto her end of the string. The student that catches the ball then states an additional positive attribute of group work and tosses the ball of string to another student while holding onto his end of the string. The class continues in this manner until all the string has been used and a web has been formed. Consider explaining how *groups are stronger when held together with a purpose.* Elaborate by pointing out that initially the string was weak and lacked purpose but how held in a group it is strong. Place a heavy object on top of the web to demonstrate how *the connections between the individual sections of string have resulted in increased strength.* Finally, pull the end of a section of the string and explain how *one person's actions (such as failing to participate on time) affects everyone in the web.* (71–72; emphasis mine)

The key impact of this exercise relies on the connections between physical sensations and linguistic metaphors described by Mark Johnson (1987). As the collaborative project is underway, or as a concluding reflection, you can return to these experiential metaphors as a way of affirming principles of productive collaboration.

SENSING THE ABSTRACT

I want to close this chapter by elaborating on the special challenge of abstract or conceptual learning: material that doesn't lend itself as easily to the use of concrete objects. If the goal of conceptual learning is to move students' cognitive perceptions from known, predictable categories into unfamiliar and more complex states of understanding, we can decrease the amount of energy such thinking requires by helping students build denser networks of conceptual associations. Synaptic networks for exteroceptive perception that we can usefully broaden and develop have been shaped by language and culture. Human cultures value various senses differently and even perceive things differently, as sensory anthropologists have documented: "The Anlo of Ghana hold that balance is a powerful sense, important in the way that vision is to Westerners. Their language contains more than fifty terms for different kinesthetic styles, and each way of walking says something about a person's moral character. . . . The Paluti of Papua New Guinea believe personal space is defined by sound. The Ongee of the Andaman Islands believe personal space is defined by smell" (Blakeslee and Blakeslee 2007, 127). A recent study of twenty diverse languages found great variability in the linguistic attention given to different senses: "While vision and sound may be privileged in English, the hierarchy of the senses, as revealed when sampling the diversity of the world's languages, is clearly not the Aristotelian one," which ranks in order of importance sight, hearing, smell, touch, taste (Majid et al. 2018, 11373). Because language—like having fifty distinct terms for styles of moving—reflects the values of a culture, teaching students new conceptual vocabulary and practicing using it helps them to build denser neural pathways to process abstract concepts.

Untranslatable words and phrases offer ways to expand our conceptual thinking, increasing what Lisa Feldman Barrett (2016) calls the "emotional granularity" of our neural networks: "Emotional granularity isn't just about having a rich vocabulary; it's about experiencing the world, and yourself, more precisely." Introducing students to untranslatable words and phrases from other languages offers them new ways of processing sensory experiences. This is a form of cognitive reappraisal: Are you walking under a canopy of trees or bathing in a healing atmosphere through *shinrin yoku* (Japanese)? Do you recognize that special twinkle in someone's eye when you first meet as *tiám* (Farsi)? How about a deep, painful, yet pleasurable longing for something that doesn't exist: the feeling of *saudade* (Portuguese)? Regional dialects and slang are also rich sources of words not found in standard English dictionaries that express human experiences with special precision. When we name an unfamiliar concept—from any culture, including the culture of a disciplinary field—and give students time to intentionally practice by applying it, repeating it, and retrieving it, we offer them one of the foundational brain benefits of education.

The arts can also play a critical role in teaching concepts through experiences rather than objects. As literary scholar G. Gabrielle Starr (2013, 92) has suggested, the arts provide a dynamic experience of learning, since each encounter with a poem or painting or performance represents a new event for the perceiver. Our brains are particularly stimulated by encountering surprise within a predictable experience; when we encounter an unexpected variation within a familiar rhythm or sound or visual landscape, our neural connections become excited. Starr calls attention to the ways we feel pleasure when we can build novel ideas onto existing experience. This principle explains the appeal of theme and variations in music composition and the bankable quality of the sequel in films, novels, or plays. It underscores the importance of building new conceptual understanding on relevant and recognizable patterns students bring into the classroom with them. It also explains why sharing multiple perspectives on the same topic can result in delightful learning: multiple translations or interpretations of the same work, a variety of approaches or interpretations of the same event or phenomenon, or different expressions of the same aesthetic style or movement. As the core material becomes more familiar, the fine differences in each approach become more appreciable.

Historical material poses special challenges because of the temporal elusiveness of the past. Teaching history requires navigating a tension between making the past feel familiar and respecting its distinctive and unrepeatable context. The latter requires students to expand their associative networks, to conceive of more complex, more varied ways of perceiving experience. The body is a critical perception machine for expanding this capability. A growing movement to "teach the archives" recognizes the effectiveness of personal artifacts and handwritten letters in overcoming the abstract distance of the past. As early modern Italian historian Lisa Kaborycha (2016, 30) testifies, "Such are the challenges facing the historian, but they are more than compensated when, in reading a woman's letter, one can hear her speaking again after four centuries of silence." Video or audio recordings from the more recent past allow us to absorb sensory signals—facial expressions and vocal sounds—that offer us important ways of connecting, even if that relationship only extends in one direction. This ability of technology to re-animate a person who's no longer alive explains why dramatic representations of historical figures can powerfully affect our sense that we know them. Daniel Day Lewis's movie portrayal of Abraham Lincoln, for example, allowed millions of people to access Lincoln's presence imaginatively by providing our eyes and ears with the sense that we encountered the real man. The impact of sensory experiences in visiting significant sites can also create a memorable sense of place, so that even physical unease creates important conceptual understanding. Historian Glenn Moore (2013, 25) offers the example of bringing students to New York City's Tenement Museum, where students were immersed in the cramped, hot, and uncomfortable rooms of the city's poor, followed by a subway journey to Coney Island, which allowed them to understand how precious these rare escapes would have been for tenement dwellers. When we can experience the physical spaces where past humans once lived, these people can become more concrete for us.

The ancient past poses daunting challenges for sensory immersion, but one museum that stands out for bringing classical antiquity to present-day visitors is the Getty Villa in Pacific Palisades, California. The Villa, free and open to the public, houses an extensive collection of ancient sculpture and mosaics, acquired over decades by the J. Paul Getty Museum and displayed in a re-created first-century Villa dei Papiri from the ruins of Herculaneum in Italy.

The gardens of the Villa showcase dozens of plants and herbs that were used in antiquity for medicinal purposes. If you take a gardens tour, you'll be provided with an audio earpiece to listen to the guide explain in hushed tones how the Romans made use of the plants' curing properties; tours here don't interrupt the natural soundscape. Guides may break off a few leaves from a selection of plants and encourage you to smell them. The scents of lavender, rosemary, boxwood, and bay laurel enhance the sights of grape-laden flowering arbors and a grand reflecting pool. A display of terracotta jars near the Inner Peristyle garden invites visitors to sniff and guess which smells were associated with special Roman holidays or everyday activities: military victory parades would have been infused with laurel, laundry day with urine detergent. The Villa pays special attention to touch as well. As you approach a secluded pergola that shelters a sculpture of the goddess Venus, a plaque labeled "Please Touch" explains that this replica was created specifically so that visitors could experience the feel of carved marble. You can run your hands

Fig. 3.1. The Inner Peristyle at the Getty Villa offers sensory delights to enhance its recreation of Roman antiquity. (Personal photograph, 2017.)

across the smooth and surprisingly soft surface of the goddess's legs and robe. The Getty strives to create a variety of learning experiences that offer pleasurable sensory memories for visitors. This strategy directly supports its mission to "encourage the appreciation and understanding of art, and its history, context, and meaning," an admirable learning goal for any educational enterprise.

Chapter Four

. . . .

LEARN TO MOVE, MOVE TO LEARN

. . . .

One of my favorite texts to include on the reading list in an early world literature survey is the brief but challenging ancient Hindu scripture the Bhagavad Gita. Like all of the foreign-language works I teach in this course, we look closely at multiple versions in English translation and listen to the sound of the original read in Sanskrit, a multisensory experience that facilitates seeking the meanings of the text through a variety of expressions. It's philosophically demanding, though, and asks readers to consider deeply personal questions about how far we might go in pursuit of our life's dharma, or sacred duty. That can be hard going at 9:30 a.m. on a Thursday in April. At some point over the years, I summoned up my courage to begin these classes with a series of gentle neck movements that I learned from practicing yoga (stretches also commonly prescribed by physical therapists), leading students through slow inhaling and exhaling as I count and model the movements. I am often nervous in anticipation of my students' reactions to doing something physical, so I explain that this practice of discipline is connected to the culture of the text we're discussing, and since I know that most of them could use a little stress relief, I hope they'll give it a try. I've never had anyone refuse, and I would contend that this physical warm-up is one of the reasons the discussions afterward are so reliably successful.

It's hard to overestimate the impact of our bodies' propensity for conserving energy. The brain's predictive, efficient, autopilot mode—always reverting to prior experience as the default reality—shapes our perceptions of every sense-able object or atmosphere and every abstract idea we consider. In general, you see and hear what your brain expects to see and hear, and your judgments about other people and new ideas are likewise constrained by what your brain knows from experience. While Nobel laureate Daniel Kahneman labels this habit of thinking as "lazy" in his important book *Thinking, Fast and Slow* (2011), we might accord it more respect. For millions of years, that precise mechanism helped human beings to live and thrive in the natural environment. It was smart to use experience to inform our actions and to be wary of the unfamiliar in a predatory world. Our bodies' instincts to conserve energy gave us the endurance to travel over vast territories on our own two feet. Snap judgment can still serve us well, especially in well-defined situations for which we've built up considerable experience to inform our instincts about likely outcomes. But in terms of critical thinking, or the ability to reflect on our own thought processes and remain open to changing our ideas, our brains are now maladaptive. Unless we can overcome our instincts to stick to what our brains think we already know, our cognitive biases will keep us warring, violent, and short-sighted in our treatment of our environment and of each other. Saving ourselves from humanity's baser instincts speaks to the purpose and power of higher education.

How can our bodies help us to overcome this over-reliance on prior experience? It takes real energy to remain open and receptive to new perceptions and ideas, and as we know, that same finite amount of energy is needed to address a lot of other issues taking up our bandwidth on any given day. The key is to look for ways that developing new physical skills and deeper awareness of our bodily perceptions can build more efficiency into our thinking processes. We can use the body to build denser, more efficient synapses for our brains to recruit in thinking. In this chapter, I explore four means of developing bodily awareness through movement to promote better critical thinking. These strategies are not typically part of academic learning and therefore may seem unorthodox and uncomfortable, but as José Bowen, in a keynote at the 2018 POD Network conference, echoed Kahneman (see Busteed 2019) on the purpose of education: "The new smart is the ability to change your mind." We must find ways to combat human brains' inclination to resist that openness.

LEARNING TO SENSE INTERNAL MOVEMENT: INTEROCEPTIVE PERCEPTION

What does it mean when we feel our hearts racing? Are we in love or excited or nervous? Over-caffeinated? If we haven't participated in regular physical exercise, we might associate a raised heart rate at the beginning of a run as emotional panic. The internal sensation feels the same, but our understanding and interpretation of it can make a big difference in how we respond. In her 2017 TED Talk "You Aren't at the Mercy of Your Emotions—Your Brain Creates Them," neuroscientist Lisa Feldman Barrett uses the example of a churning stomach; when we're inside an aromatic bakery, we interpret this signal as hunger, but in a hospital waiting room, the same signal might suggest dread. Individuals' levels of awareness of internal sensations (interoceptive awareness, or IA) has become a topic of increasing interest in neuroscience and cognitive psychology. Researcher Wolf Mehling (2016, 2) defines metacognitive awareness as "a mental condition that allows individuals to disidentify and disengage from their own emotions and related bodily feelings, enabling them to observe these as dynamic phenomena within their personal experience, without thinking or believing that these emotions and feelings are self-defining." Like other kinds of metacognitive awareness, interoceptive perception involves an ability to monitor and evaluate one's own thinking and feeling—in this case, about internal sensations.

Scientists have developed questionnaires to assess degrees of IA; the Multidimensional Assessment of Interoceptive Awareness (Osher Center 2018; MAIA-2) is a set of thirty-seven questions that probe an individual's perceived sensitivity to bodily sensations (both pleasant and painful), as well as how the test-taker processes these sensations: do they lead to worry and fear, or are they sought out as valid sources of information for interpretation and regulation? Studies on interoceptive perception (see Garfinkel et al. 2014, 66) have demonstrated that people with a high degree of confidence in their perceptions are not necessarily more accurate, so that each variable in perception—metacognitive awareness, subjective sensitivity, and objective accuracy—should be regarded independently. In particular, our sensitivity to heartbeats, breathing rates, and gastrointestinal activity can be maladaptive when leading to hypervigilance and catastrophic thinking or highly beneficial when leading to greater self-regulation of emotions and attention (see Mehling 2016, 3). The goal of increasing one's IA isn't to become more accurate but rather to gain more control over our attention to internal signals and to better regulate our responses to them. In the classroom, that means helping students to develop confidence about their abilities to concentrate on learning and to perform well under the pressure of tests and presentations.

Recently, I made an unexpected discovery about how bodies can shape minds: as I waited for my turn on a meeting agenda to present an idea to a roomful of colleagues, I felt myself trembling, and unable to calm down inside. It surprised me to notice how nervous I was becoming, and I tried to settle down by considering a new interpretation of the jitters, "reframing" my shaking as excitement. After all, I had something positive and useful to share. But that didn't stop the quivering, either. A few minutes later, I noticed that the air temperature of the room was well below normal. Aha! I was shivering from the cold, which I first misinterpreted as nerves, then unsuccessfully tried to reframe as excitement. The external conditions of the environment were affecting my attention and readiness to contribute to the conversation. That sudden recognition changed my level of confidence because I could attribute my shaking to a chill, not a fear of public speaking. "Whether we view our racing heart and sweaty palms as a sign of excitement or anxiety has a lot to do with whether we will clutch or choke," explains cognitive scientist Sian Beilock (2015, 178). And as we know from embodied cognition principle 3, the boundary line of our bodies can extend to our surrounding environment. The skill of cognitive reappraisal, or the ability to assess your own state of understanding and apply alternative interpretations to change your response, empowers our cognitive development and states of growth.

Spending a few minutes of time in class to help students develop greater IA shows that you are invested in helping them to succeed and to confidently perform at their best.

Three activities have shown potential to improve IA: body scan exercises, breathing meditation, and power-posing. One recent study involved intensive interventions, beginning with an initial three-day retreat and followed by three months of daily practice and a weekly class led by expert guides. The study authors describe its method: "During the BoS [body scan] (e.g., Kabat-Zinn, 1990), participants systematically guide their attention to different parts of their body, starting with their toes and ending up on the top of their heads. Participants are asked to attend to the sensations in the various body parts they are focusing on. In the BrM [breathing meditation] (e.g., Wallace, 2006), participants are asked to focus on the sensations of their breathing. In both practices, participants are asked to resume their interoceptive focus on body parts or their breath, whenever attention has strayed" (Bornemann et al. 2015, 4). Both body scan and breathing meditation practices produced significant results in subjects' reported abilities to "direct attention toward their bodies (Attention Regulation) and . . . make use of these abilities to regulate distress (Self-Regulation) and to gain insight into their emotional-motivational state (Body Listening)," as measured by the MAIA (Bornemann et al. 2015, 9). Body scans and breathing meditations are simple enough to learn, however, even without a period of intensive training. Free apps and websites such as *Greater Good in Action* can guide you and your students through these exercises together in class, and you might assign time to repeat them outside of class as homework. *Greater Good*'s Mindful Breathing exercise (2020) can take just a few minutes, as described here:

> Sometimes, especially when trying to calm yourself in a stressful moment, it might help to start by taking an exaggerated breath: a deep inhale through your nostrils (3 seconds), hold

your breath (2 seconds), and a long exhale through your mouth (4 seconds). Otherwise, simply observe each breath without trying to adjust it; it may help to focus on the rise and fall of your chest or the sensation through your nostrils. As you do so, you may find that your mind wanders, distracted by thoughts or bodily sensations. That's OK. Just notice that this is happening and gently bring your attention back to your breath.

One particularly clever integration of a breathing exercise with academic content has been developed by environmental scientist Russell Fielding. He shared this exercise with *Chronicle of Higher Education* readers of the "Teaching" newsletter: "To help students comprehend the timescale at which climate change affects glaciers and glacially dependent landscapes . . . I incorporate a meditation-based breathing exercise, in which each deep inhale represents a winter of snow and ice accumulation, each exhale represents a summer of ablation or melting, and the relative pace and depth of breathing—directed by silent visual clues—changes according to the climatic conditions being enacted. After such an exercise in my introductory course, one student, slightly out of breath, remarked that he now knew 'how a melting glacier feels' " (quoted in McMurtrie 2019).

Power-posing is a practice that has endured a bit of scholarly controversy since first introduced by social psychologist Amy Cuddy in 2010; her conclusion was initially discounted after several studies were not able to replicate its full results, but newer studies are again demonstrating that subjects primed by empowering language and body gestures do experience an immediate but temporary increase in self-focus, related to IA (see Weineck et al. 2019; Kunstmann et al. 2016). What's a power pose? In general, these are body postures that expand the amount of social space we use by opening our limbs. Standing with our arms raised above our heads in the "victory" gesture of a race winner or goal-scoring athlete, or standing hands on hips with a wide-leg stance, or sitting with legs stretched out or knees spread wide are examples of ways we communicate confidence and subjective feelings of power. Taking these postures appears to signal confidence not only to others, but to ourselves, through IA. The positive effect of power-posing has been shown to be particularly helpful for women, which suggests one concrete strategy for mitigating stereotype threat in disciplines where women are underrepresented. Research on the link between behavior and perception has shown that "stereotypic movements activate the corresponding stereotype" (Mussweiler 2006). While it might seem weird as a classroom practice before beginning a test or delivering presentations, it doesn't take much time, and will communicate to students that we want them to perform at their best.

SENSING MOVEMENT THROUGH SPACE: PROPRIOCEPTIVE PERCEPTION

Proprioception, which allows us to detect the movement and position of our own body, may be the most fascinating of the various perceptive abilities. It makes us aware of how we are integrated within the space of our environment, how we are positioned in relation to other people, and how our bodies signal our presence to others as well as to ourselves. Activities that help us to practice our sense of balance and develop a better awareness of the position of our limbs increase our proprioceptive sense, like dance and martial arts (including yoga and tai chi), as well as sports that require handling a ball or wielding a bat, stick, or racket. "Any motor skill more complicated than walking has to be learned," points out John

Ratey (2008, 56), "and thus it challenges the brain. At first you're awkward and flail a little bit, but then as the circuits linking the cerebellum, basal ganglia, and prefrontal cortex get humming, your movements become more precise. With the repetition, you're also creating thicker myelin around the nerve fibers, which improves the quality and the speed of the signals, and, in turn, the circuit's efficiency." As we know, increasing the efficiency of brain functions is directly beneficial for learning. Ratey is a major proponent of running as a means to increasing brain performance; running, he argues, "defines us" as humans and may even explain our special relationships with other species with whom we can run together: dogs and horses (2014, 24).

The better our own proprioceptive perception, the better we also understand and appreciate the performance of physical skills in others. When we watch others play instruments or perform athletic skills that we ourselves have practiced, the corresponding areas of our brains become activated in a way that does not happen in those who have never tried the activity. According to Blakeslee and Blakeslee (2007, 169), "When pianists listen to someone else's piano performance, the finger areas in their primary and premotor cortex increase above their baseline activity. . . . The same thing does not happen in the brains of nonmusicians. While they certainly can appreciate the music deeply, their experience is inevitably shallower than the pianist's in at least one way, because they are not experiencing what it is like to actually produce it." The implications of this picture are enormous: learning new physical skills allows us to perceive the world differently, and in a deeper way. The broader and more diverse our range of experiences, the denser and more efficient our neural networks become. We can encourage students to pursue new physical activities and skills explicitly for brain growth. For example, "Neurobics (neuron + aerobics)," as coined by Cia Verschelden (2017, 72) in her book *Bandwidth Recovery*, are recommended as "stretching exercises to increase oxygen and give our brain's neurons more life by experiencing or participating in some new activity, situation, or event. When we stretch our mind, it never returns to its previous shape." Ideas such as spending one day walking backward or using your nondominant hand are among her neurobics that engage the body.

Using our hands as affordances through gesture allows us to connect motor associations with new conceptual language. By giving abstract words an embodied existence, gestures can "reinforce the sensorimotor representation of a word or a phrase, making it resistant to decay" (Macedonia et al. 2012). Gesturing may include forming emblems, like thumbs-up, to serve as substitutes for words; pointing with our fingers or heads or eyes to refer to seen or imagined objects; or performing metaphorical actions to give shape to abstract concepts (see Tversky 2019, 116–19). Foreign-language educators recommend adopting gesture as a classroom learning tool; intentional body movement supports the learning of any new terminology or conceptual language (see Fiorella et al. 2015). Research on the impact of gestures for learning has demonstrated the fundamental role of the body in mathematical reasoning. Deborah Moore-Russo and her colleagues (2014) performed a fascinating case study analysis of twelve doctoral students from a large U.S. research university working on a "non-trivial" proof. After observing and coding the gestures of the mathematicians, they conclude that expert mathematical work "is a richly embodied practice that involves inscribing and manipulating notations, interacting with those notations through speech and gesture, and using the body to enact the meanings of mathematical ideas. By including gesture in the analysis, we take the mathematician's body seriously as a semiotic resource in the creation and communication of mathematical content. Seen in this light, mathematical proof is no longer an abstract product but is instead a dynamic practice, a human activity that involves talking, inscribing, and, crucially, gesturing: Mathematics is manual labor" (Moore-Russo et al. 2014, 222). Research in mathematics education at the primary school level has demonstrated that mathematical thinking can be critically affected through developing the skill of finger discrimination, or the proprioception of each distinct finger. Training that increases finger discrimination has been shown to directly improve numerical reasoning, and better predicts future performance in math than cognitive tests (see Gracia-Bafalluy et al. 2008). Our own hands serve as key affordances for off-loading cognitive tasks.

The gesture of the raised hand is a particularly powerful signal to ourselves and to others in the classroom setting. It's a modified version of the power pose that registers our presence by calling attention to our right to speak. Cathy N. Davidson (2015) recounts a classroom practice of the science fiction writer Samuel R. Delany, who required all students in his class to raise their hands in response to a question: "Whether one knows the answer, doesn't know, or doesn't understand the question, [Delany] insists that every hand go up and he calls on someone to answer at random. They can then either offer an answer, articulate something about the question they don't understand, or say they don't know the answer and that they want to hear what Person X has to say about it. In any case, they represent themselves as present, as a participant, by that boldly raised hand (even if the answer is unknown) that says: I. Am. Here." Delany had come to this awareness after contemplating the cumulative

Fig. 4.1. Raising one's hand signals presence, to others and to oneself. (Photograph courtesy of Sebastiaan ter Burg. Posted on Flickr in Wikimania 2014 album, August 9, 2014. CC-BY 2.0 license.)

effect on students of spending years in classrooms without having raised a hand. Remaining still and unrecognized results in a "violence of silence" for learners. The power dynamic of the classroom matters here, and shaking up the traditional structure of classroom conversation so that more than one voice can speak at a time works just as effectively to empower learners. Nonetheless, raising one's hand confidently does communicate something meaningful to ourselves through proprioception.

HANDLING AND MOVING THINGS: MANIPULATION

In the last chapter, I introduced touch as a particularly important sense for learning. Object-Based Learning can be extended to almost any discipline as a way of bringing concrete experience to the objects of our study. Even watching a teacher handle an object, using positively associated language to describe it, can induce pleasure in viewers' brains and thereby increase motivation to learn (see McCabe et al. 2008). I'd bet that many of us experienced childhood teacher-envy because we wanted to hold that stack of papers, that clipboard, that plastic model of the heart. The importance of object manipulation for learning means that we should think carefully about everything students handle and about their perceptions of objects in our classroom: not just instruments, tools, specimens, or artifacts, but the classroom chalk or whiteboard markers and erasers, their computer keyboards, and the format of their assigned reading. How do we know when students feel alienated from the objects in their learning spaces? I've walked into classrooms to find a dozen students sitting in the near-dark because no one wanted to brave flipping on the light switches. We do our students a disservice when we teach them that basic classroom furniture is off-limits to touch or move. Have a productive conversation about how students perceive the environment in the classroom: How can everyone contribute to creating an environment conducive to the class activities? What time and energy are needed to set up your classroom and then reset it for others who will use the same space later?

Writing implements are key affordances for learning, which we know as a principle of embodied cognition. Anecdotal evidence of my own and from colleagues suggests that students are more willing to write down tentative ideas when they're provided with whiteboards; the medium is so forgiving, it makes risk-taking easier. Colored markers with whiteboards and/or giant sticky notes can create a classroom that visually explodes with ideas. Research on notetaking with pen and paper versus typing shows varied results for impact on students' comprehension and recall. Both are kinds of manipulation, and individual students have differing levels of skill in each. Guidance about the purpose and goals for notes matters, as does the use students make of them afterward (see Kuepper-Tetzel 2019). Some studies suggest that typing may carry a subtle cognitive bias for words that we can produce more easily on the standard QWERTY standard keyboard (see Jasmin et al. 2012; Beilock et al. 2007). Pen-and-paper notes are generally less dense but can more easily incorporate drawings and concept maps, which invite students to process their understanding as they shape their notes. A growing number of guidebooks and how-to videos are aimed at teaching beginners how to sketchnote, creating visual illustrations as a way of notetaking. Linda J. Breslin and Kristen E. Gregory, in a "Draw-and-Write Method" session of the 2019 Transformative Learning Conference, testified to the freedom offered by "college" crayons or colored pencils, which help to promote risk-taking through association of the tool with playfulness. The combination of taking notes and observing others doing the same can provide transparency for sharing effective approaches. If you've got a mini-lecture to deliver or a podcast to share, assign students to take notes on classroom whiteboards—including drawings or maps of the ideas—as they listen. At the conclusion of the talk, they'll have easily visible references to share and compare what they found most important and interesting. Snapping photos of the boards allows them to save the work for future reference.

Avid readers often testify to the satisfying texture of pages in a book; personally, I miss the pleasure of handling a big, fat Sunday newspaper. Digital texts are fast, efficient, convenient, and increasingly easy to navigate and annotate, but the importance of manipulation in human learning suggests that we should carefully consider how students will consume the reading we assign. Open educational resources allow for equitable access to materials and enable students to read online for free or in print for the cost of the paper and ink. As an early adopter of open educational resources for my classroom, I learned quickly that a shift to digital material necessitated extra class time for us to discuss and practice navigating and annotating various digital formats. It's also important to support students who express a preference for reading and marking in print. Because strategies for reading differ across disciplines, these conversations are likely to raise issues worth having in every classroom: What do you expect students to do, exactly, when they read? What specific goals should they be pursuing by reading the assigned material: acquiring new terminology? applying conceptual knowledge to examples or case studies? identifying the writer's characteristic sentence structures or ability to achieve linguistic nuance? Keith Hjortshoj's (2009, 32) text for first-year students, *The Transition to College Writing*, helpfully recommends teaching "predatory reading," a metaphor for a range of strategies that allow students to consume what they need from assigned texts. Effective learning from reading makes it absolutely critical that students be able to manipulate it easily and ideally with pleasure, so that the text is marked by the encounter with their own eyes or ears.

MOVING TO LEARN: LOCOMOTION

While I agree with *How Humans Learn* (2018b) author Josh Eyler that "active learning" is becoming a buzzword, it might help to clarify what active learning means by emphasizing a physical component. Eyler (2018a) suggests that "successful teaching is not about activity, per se. It's about choosing strategies that are most connected to how people learn." Yet embodied cognition science suggests that we learn best when we're moving; we have a pervasive, multigenerational heritage of sedentary learning to overcome. Here's a challenge: take any particular plan for a day of class (the material you need to address, any discussions or activities you want to include) and see how many times you can incorporate getting students away from their desks. Can you get students circulating through a number of different places in the room, or outside of it? In a traditional classroom, locomotion happens twice: when students enter and find their desks, then again when they leave. But as we know from embodied cognition principle 1, our bodies are always in motion. We are built to move and to think while moving. Rather than taking breaks to stretch, we'd be better off to need breaks to sit. Our spines need movement to prevent the chronic back pain too many people suffer from a lifetime of sedentary school and work conditions. If we followed the exhortations of environmental humanist Vybarr Cregan-Reid (2018a), governments would declare as hazardous to public health any school or job that required remaining seated for the majority of the day.

Of the many ways to inject more locomotive movement into our classes, here are a few starter ideas to adopt or modify.

The Bounce

Borrowed from the November Project, a national movement to bring people together for free, outdoor, early morning exercise that builds local community as well as health, this opening ritual is described by bloggers Lauren Carter (2017) and Elizabeth MacKenzie as "the act of jumping up and down, sometimes a little and sometimes a lot and creating

this wave of excitement and hype, definitely the hype."
November Project leaders lead the Bounce with a call-and-
response yell that you may or may not choose to include.
But as they testify, even a gentle up and down, at whatever
level of mobility is available to us, can become a favorite
way to begin sharing time together. Daniel Braun, Carolyn
Ives, and Paul Martin at MacEwan University in Edmonton,
Alberta, participated with colleagues in November Project
workouts as a faculty learning community to rethink how
they create a sense of community in their classes. Opening
your classes with the Bounce violates academic norms for
all the right reasons: it takes as little as thirty seconds, gets
critical oxygen and nutrients circulating to the brain, and
achieves the critical effect of shaking up students' expectations for whatever else might happen in the ensuing hour.

Mapping the Room

We can usefully inform our own priorities for time in class
by polling students about their prior knowledge of the topic
or about their developing understanding. We also know that
the best kinds of questions evade simple yes or no or right
or wrong answers. Even questions with correct or "better"
answers can be further probed by asking students to share
their levels of confidence or certainty. While clickers are a
technically convenient tool (and phones can now be easily
converted for this purpose with free quizzing apps), why not
involve the whole body? Break up the room into quadrants
and pose a question with four possible answers and corresponding positions to move toward; alternatively, you might
propose an invisible axis running down the middle of the
room, with opposing concepts at each end of the spectrum.
You might ask several related questions in a quick series

to watch how the movement in the room reflects students' thinking and their levels of confidence about their answers. You can prompt further discussion among groups in each self-selected area or among the whole class about why they've taken that position. Students are more likely to recall the discussion and their own stance due to a physical experience of deliberately occupying a specific place. Beyond getting everyone away from their desks, this exercise has the advantage of involving every student. You have to take a stand, literally.

Move-and-Think / Meet-and-Pair / Stay-and-Share

It's been more than twenty years since Harvard physicist Eric Mazur (1997) and the Derek Bok Center for Teaching and Learning launched *Peer Instruction*. For many faculty, think/pair/share is now standard practice. But the insights of embodied cognition suggest it's now time for Peer Instruction 2.0, which removes sitting still from the three-step equation.

1. We know that movement promotes better idea-invention, so why not begin with a Move-and-Think? Send students out for a quick loop around the quad to discuss preliminary responses to a question, or assign a question in advance to mull over as they make their way to class.

2. Before anyone has claimed a desk, ask students to form facing inner and outer circles for Meet-and-Pair exercise. The University of the Pacific's Center for Teaching and Learning calls this "speed thinking": set a timer for members of only one of the circles (inner or outer) to briefly share their answers to the question; the challenge of the other circle members is to maintain eye contact and to remain silent in order to develop listening skills. For the second round, ask the listeners to summarize

for their partners what they've heard and understood, or give the other circle's members their own chance to answer the question. You can continue rotating the circles to form new partnerships for follow-up questions. If students don't all know each other's names, include introducing themselves as part of the instructions. University of the Pacific faculty developers Leslie Bayers and Lott Hill (2019) report that "speed thinking is not only an animated activity that can productively boost energy and engagement in class, but also a practice that can help students build [students'] contemplative listening endurance."

3. To pull together the discussion and offer students a chance to reflect on what they've discovered together, have them remain away from their desks and spread around the perimeter of the room, so that it's possible for the whole class to see and hear a speaker. Stay-and-Share offers student volunteers (or those called upon) to voice a position that's been informed and refined by multiple other students.

While moving around the room requires more space, it can take as much or as little time as you choose and invigorates peer instruction. Everyone has participated and spoken, a sense of belonging has been promoted through eye contact, and the focus has remained on the content of your material.

Dance and Unplanned Movement

Dance is perhaps the oldest, most primal form of creative expression, and its power to communicate is underappreciated, at best. New work that integrates cognitive psychology and dance is showing that humans can perceive quite complex emotions as signaled through dance movements and that we do this by applying our predictive expectations to our observations of others' body movements (see Gervasio 2012). Dance psychologist Peter Lovatt describes an experiment that asked twenty-three choreographers to design and perform a three-minute dance based on a single, emotion-related word: "I put on a show for 23 nights where I talked about the science of emotion recognition and then invited a different choreographer to come on stage to demonstrate their dance. Afterwards we asked the audience to describe the emotions they thought were being conveyed in the dance. The findings were astounding. The audience always got it right, even for the most complex emotional states" (quoted in Kinman 2014, 347). This ability to decipher meaning from body movement extends to most humans' innate sense of what "natural" human movement looks like. Published studies on body movement perception have informed the development of reflective clothing for runners, notably increasing pedestrian safety (see Cutting 2013). Our ability to perceive body movement also explains why director Peter Jackson and his team of documentary filmmakers were able to correct the speed of choppy World War I footage without any recorded settings to help guide the adjustments for their film *They Shall Not Grow Old* (2018). "You realize, for 100 years, we've seen these guys at a super-fast speed, full of grain, jerky, jumping up and down, which has completely disguised their humanity," said Jackson. "But the transformation happens when you take away all that damage and get [the soldiers] moving at a normal human speed. They become real people again" (quoted in Sims 2018).

Dance is active movement that improves our own brain functioning in general. Lovatt's dance psychology lab at the University of Hertfordshire has been able to show that rhythmic, planned dances (like "line dances" with synchronized moves) speed up our brain processing, so that we can perform convergent thinking tasks like math calculation more quickly. But for better creative, improvisational, divergent thinking tasks, planned movement doesn't help—for that, we can improve our thinking through unplanned, free-form dance movement. Lovatt (2018, 51) explains the connection: "The reason improvised dance helps us to be more creative is because it is helping us to break away from set patterns of movement, which in turn helps us to break away from set patterns of thinking." In his popular personal appearances and TED Talk, Lovatt leads people through a set of dances they join from their places in the audience; it's a persuasive demonstration of both our primal enjoyment of dancing and of the impact a short few minutes of free-form dance has on our energy levels and creative thinking. When was the last time you and your students let loose with a little loud music? You can tell them, it's science.

Transparency about why we're asking students to participate in these unorthodox exercises is absolutely key to their success. Students need to know that moving their bodies can improve the functioning of their brains. They need to have an explanation of what the activity will involve, encouragement to try, and alternative options if they're not yet ready. As Lott Hill and Leslie Bayers (personal communication, 2019) have found, resistance to movement can become part of a conversation about the difference between "uncomfortable" and "unsafe." They recommend following up supported risk-taking with a debrief to ask participants afterward how it felt for them. One unavoidable issue with locomotion as a classroom strategy: incorporating bodily movement may work against an inclusive environment for students with alternative mobility methods. We cannot ignore the presence of students who use assistive devices or move with more difficulty because of obesity, chronic illness, or age. We want to promote a sense of belonging. Many of these exercises could be done while remaining seated—a gentler, upper-body-only kind of locomotion—and I encourage teachers to support and affirm students' abilities at any level.

Moving around, handling things, sensing the position of our bodies in space, and sensing motion internally: these are the ways that our bodies work to understand the world. As Guy Claxton (2015, 91) posits, the integration of interoceptive messages from our tissues and organs, our sensory impressions, and the predictions based on our prior experiences function like a succession of momentary waves: "Each momentary wave is not separated from the moment before and the moment after. Like a real wave, it has both a leading and a trailing edge. It is simultaneously rising, existing, and fading. In the rising are expectations and predictions of what the future may bring, and in the fading are echoes of the confirmations and surprises that arose from moments that have just been. (*So the fading edge is where learning happens*)" (emphasis mine). Unlike the dynamic experience of learning through momentary waves, learning in the industrial age has focused on stasis: we sit still, listen, and perform some kind of absorption that we imagine takes place entirely within the confines of our skulls. That stasis has informed our sense of educational norms, and the infrastructure of classroom buildings reflects it. But neuroscience is revealing that learning is in fact an embodied process, so that the way we use our bodies changes the way we think. "Unconventional" may seem an understatement when we consider how radically this should prompt us to reconceive classroom practice. On the other hand, our bodies are accessible and inexpensive technology, and the potential rewards for engaging them are well worth trying.

Part Three

. . . .

BREAK THROUGH BOUNDARIES

Chapter Five

....

MOVE AROUND TOGETHER

....

If human beings are the Swiss Army knives of motion, our social skills are likewise much more complex and adaptable than those of other earthly creatures. Bees, ants, and termites can form quite large societies and work in a coordinated manner to accomplish difficult tasks. This impressive coordination is only possible because each member of the society knows and performs a scripted role. Mammals can cooperate more flexibly, but not in large numbers; they need to know and trust each other member of the group. But as historian Yuval Noah Harari (2016) notes, only humans are capable of working together in large numbers and in flexible ways, which has made possible our coordinated efforts to form societies, to communicate and trade among each other, and in general, to dominate the planet. There's no question that sociality is one of humans' unique and premier strengths. But like worker ants with simple, prescribed roles, students in industrial-age education have been expected to perform individual labors that satisfy predetermined outcomes. It's clear that this model isn't preparing them to deal with unscripted problems that require collaboration to solve.

Letting go of these rigid roles to empower students as co-creators of shared knowledge and skills is much messier and carries a greater risk of failure.

Dozens of challenging factors come into play when any group of human beings are brought together to accomplish a shared task. Facilitating collaborative work can feel like feeding kids vegetables: we know these things are good for them, they'll benefit long-term from wide and varied exposure, and they can develop genuine taste and enjoyment for the experience. But it's not the easiest choice. Canned lectures, Scantron exams, and publishers' course packs offer much easier ways to deliver our subject matter and to test students' understanding of it. As stand-up comedian Jim Gaffigan (2005, 46:03) jokes in *Beyond the Pale*, "Should I have this salad for twelve dollars or these eight hamburgers for a nickel? Sorry, salad!" This is the hard reality of teaching for long-term, transformative development: hands-on, active, collaborative learning is simply harder to plan, to implement, and to assess. In her book *The Spark of Learning*, psychologist and educational researcher Sarah Rose Cavanagh (2016, 200–202) describes the uneven division of labor that often mars small group work, and offers practical strategies for assigning and monitoring it effectively. Over the past few decades, practitioners of collaborative pedagogy have developed a wealth of strategies to overcome some of its inherent challenges. There are entire books (discipline-specific and cross-disciplinary), articles, videos, and websites devoted to collaborative learning. My purpose here is not to review the existing literature but to explore how paying attention to the body offers us a new way of approaching the complexity of collaboration.

Since prior experiences are so central to shaping perception, as we know from embodied cognition science, bad experiences with group work likely poison subsequent attempts. If certain behaviors seem like familiar or predictable roles (the dominator? the slacker? the ghost?), that makes it more likely that the group's figurative wagon wheels will roll into these deep ruts. That's true for teachers as well as for students. We need as many or more positive experiences as negative ones to overcome inherently low expectations for group work. Bad experiences with collaborative learning have also shaped the views of those who object to its presumed poor fit for introverted students and teachers. I sympathize with this point of view, and I will argue here that our practices of collaborative learning haven't attended carefully enough to building the relationships that make it rewarding. The long-range impact of collaborative learning remains relatively unexamined, as Elizabeth Barkley and colleagues identify in *Collaborative Learning Techniques* (2014, 32): for example, are there risks for students when group work goes poorly? And what are the effects of collaborative learning on teachers? These are important, meaningful questions, considering how often group work can go poorly and its inherent demands on teachers. In this chapter, I want to establish why collaborative work is exceptionally complex, why it matters so much to students' learning, and how paying attention to the body offers us another way to manage effective collaboration.

Our ever-moving bodies prize efficiency, as we know from embodied cognition principle 2; the brain's default prediction mode shapes our sensory perceptions and thus our cognitive understanding. This is especially relevant to our perceptions of other people. We bring all of our prior experiences with various kinds of people, including real people and fictional representations, to bear on our interactions with a new person. It makes sense from an evolutionary point of view that we would want to use this predictive capacity to anticipate a new person's actions or behavior: should we be wary? Is this person a potential affordance to our own actions or behavior (embodied cognition principle 3)? But the drawbacks can be terribly detrimental to an authentic interaction with a new person, whose qualities may differ significantly from our predictions. This is the realm of inherent bias and the reason we can't completely eradicate it. People interacting in a society affect each other's embodied ecosystems (embodied cognition principle 4) like a feedback loop: we are constantly monitoring others' responses to ourselves, and that informs our behavior toward others. We shape each other's ecosystems in concrete physical ways, eliciting fight-or-flight rushes of cortisol that cause our blood pressure to spike or feel-good surges of oxytocin that reduce stress.

Our perceptions are shaped by everything we can sense about other people: the way they look, move, sound, smell, and even in some cases the way their bodies feel to us. Our senses draw from experience as a default mode to predict how others are likely to behave. Sometimes our sensory input quickly and smoothly confirms our predictions. But when we get conflicting signals, our brains work to interpret them in a way that will resolve the dissonance. Neuroscientist Lisa Feldman Barrett (2017a, 65) likens the brain at this moment to a scientist whose data doesn't match its hypothesis: "It can be a responsible scientist and change its predictions to respond to the data. Your brain can also be a biased scientist and selectively choose the data that fits the hypotheses, ignoring everything else. Your brain can also be an unscrupulous scientist and ignore the data altogether, maintaining that its predictions are the reality." Biased and unscrupulous brains are less demanding users of energy and therefore can override our capacity to remain open and curious—in other words, to learn. The unscrupulous brain at work has been studied by psychologists and linguists, for example, in experiments that test listeners' comprehension of familiar and unfamiliar voices. Familiar voices are heard as more intelligible to listeners (see Holmes et al. 2018). Unfamiliar voices—including those belonging to speakers we perceive as unfamiliar through sight—can measurably affect our comprehension of that voice.

In a seminal experiment, U.S. undergraduate students listened to a recorded lecture made by a native English speaker with a socially neutral accent; half of the group viewed a still photo of an Asian face as the purported lecturer, and the other half was shown a white face. Tests of their recall of the lecture material afterward showed that students' expectations of the "Asian" speaker's intelligibility impaired their ability to absorb the material (Kang and Rubin 2009). The students' eyes predicted having trouble understanding an Asian speaker, and their ears did. In actual classes taught by non-native English speakers, students frequently blame a teacher's accent for any difficulty they experience with understanding the material. To mitigate this phenomenon, the study authors recommend facilitating group problem-solving exercises as "social-psychological inoculations against linguistic stereotyping" (Kang et al. 2015, 699). Working together to complete a shared task involves natural, conversational exchange that builds familiarity with accented speech. Neuroscience offers another way to describe this intervention: an "inoculation" conversation offers the brain new experience from which to draw. Our ability to process unfamiliar voices depends on the diversity of experiences we bring to that situation; our brains can more quickly and efficiently process signals for which we've got prior experience—so the denser our network of prior experiences, the easier.

If listening to an unfamiliar voice can lead to real difficulties, let us pause for a moment to consider the dozens of other physical factors that may affect successful collaborative learning. Our interactions with others will involve their perceptions of our speech, our dress, our grooming, our posture, our gestures, our gait, the smell of our breath or skin, our facial expressions, and perhaps the feel of our hands. In turn, we're making all of the same interpretations of others, influenced by the amount of sleep we're getting and what we're feeding ourselves, plus the sum total of our own social experiences. Interpersonal dynamics may appear doomed by "a trash can fire of personalities," as educational researcher Eddie Watson joked during a workshop at my university. (Knowing laughs confirmed this experience of assigning group work.) It's critical for productive groups to develop a sense of shared purpose or identity, and that's tougher when our perceptions of others suggest that we don't share much in common. Ironically, a group that forms a quick sense of common identity can pose a different challenge: there's the potential for their energy to be misdirected. A group who has developed a tight sense of shared identity might be inclined to lead a mutiny against the teacher or undermine other groups' willingness to participate. The remedy for all of these difficulties is challenging: as teacher and students together, we have to acknowledge and monitor our individual responses to each other, to be as self-aware as possible about the range of prior experiences provided by our respective upbringings, our cultural influences, and our most emotionally resonant relationships, then seek to broaden and diversify this range of experiences. This chapter offers some ideas for teaching, modeling, and reinforcing self-awareness and for diversifying students' social experiences.

WHAT SCIENCE TELLS US ABOUT HUMANS' RESPONSES TO POSITIVE SOCIAL INTERACTIONS

The social dimension of a physical classroom is enormously important. Research on student seating in a lecture hall has explored the impact on academic performance of the physical environment, including the size and density of the room, and the patterns of grade distribution among students who locate themselves toward the front or back, center or aisle (see Perkins and Wieman 2005). Studies have also been done on the motives of students to choose certain areas to sit, such as physical needs (left-handed desks, mobility issues, clear line of sight), a desire to be seen or to hide, and a wish to sit together with friends or acquaintances (see Losonczy-Marshall and Marshall 2013). Because academic performance has been shown to frequently correspond with seating clusters in a lecture hall, researchers (see Smith et al. 2018) recommend that think/pair/share exercises be conducted between partners sitting in rows directly in front or behind one another, and that student response systems (clickers) be used to check whole-class understanding of key lecture points. Another intervention, interestingly, involves thwarting the static environment of the lecture hall altogether: researchers recommend providing opportunities to help students feel comfortable interacting with diverse others from the start. Move-and-think/meet-and-pair/stay-and-share (described in the last chapter), for example, mix up the room, making it less likely that students will cluster in uneven attainment groups. Scholarly work on how to improve learning outcomes in these kinds of spaces certainly addresses a practical need, but I think it's worth pointing out that the lecture hall space itself is creating an obstacle for some students' learning.

As researchers describe the effect on human beings of interacting in any social space, even small physical gestures of others shape our own feelings of belonging:

> Someone touches us on the shoulder, calls our name, or a passing stranger glances at us, and this is a catalyst, a rapid switching mechanism (Iberall & Soodak, 1987) for switching from an autonomous individual mode of action to being pulled temporarily into a "social eddy" with another, a dynamic patterning, a dance that includes rich nonverbal (and perhaps verbal) behavior, responsivity, mutuality, and coordination of behavior. These social interactions are so brief and spontaneous that we take little note of them, but we may carry their impact with us—they may make us feel attractive, important, stupid, uninteresting, threatened or safe. (Marsh et al. 2009, 1222)

Being pulled into a "social eddy" of group work can drain the energies of more introverted people because there are so many verbal and nonverbal signals to monitor. The work of that dance becomes easier, however, as the behavior of other members of the group becomes better known and therefore demands less energy to predict. As Susan Cain's important book *Quiet* (2012) establishes, more introverted people are not antisocial but prefer to socialize more substantively with fewer others. This preference explains why collaborative learning can be more successful when groups are maintained over a longer period of time, enabling students to develop sustained relationships. The creation of positive and productive relationships, however, matters significantly in longer-term groups. The impact of repeated interactions over time signals to us how others perceive and respond to us, and not only shapes our self-perception but can impact our brains and physical health.

A sense of belonging offers students the chance to recover needed bandwidth for learning. Even for introverts, positive social interactions have been shown to enhance experiences and lead to an improved overall sense of well-being. Psychologists Nicholas Epley and Juliana Schroeder (2014) conducted a series of nine experiments that asked people to interact with strangers and report both their prior expectations and resulting feelings about how pleasant the experience would be. Most participants in the experiments didn't anticipate that they would enjoy interacting with strangers but reported afterward that their social interaction had enhanced an experience (in this case, of commuting on public transportation) normally undertaken in solitude. The study shows that many of us routinely undervalue social connection. Embodied cognition science posits that we shape each other's ecosystems, and the work of Epley and Schroeder (1988, 1995) suggests that social and cultural norms have led us to behave in ways that actually work against our own benefit:

> Misunderstanding the consequences of social connection comes, at least in part, from barriers to engaging in conversation rather than from biased memory for past conversations or biased imagination for conversations once engaged. Solitude seems preferable to connecting with a stranger, it appears, because people interpret others' actions as signs of disinterest and therefore do not engage in the very conversations that would correct their expectations. . . . People do not so much have a preference for solitude in the presence of

strangers as they do a fear of the negative consequences that
might come from attempted interactions.

In other words, prior experience doesn't hamper our willingness to interact with strangers. Because the essential quality
of strangers is their unknown-ness, our brains can't easily
apply past positive experiences with strangers to predict
positive new ones. Culture and perception of the environment also affect our expectations; I can testify to this effect. During morning runs in a neighborhood park with my
partner, Nick, we exchange greetings with other walkers
and runners of all ages, body types, racial and ethnic identities, and socioeconomic statuses. Making an effort to pant
"Morning!" regardless of perceived differences does enhance
our sense of connection and belonging.

Humans are fundamentally social animals, and we use
each other as affordances for action. Social support makes
tasks seem easier: a hill doesn't seem as steep when we're
climbing with others, and that effect increases with the
closeness of the relationship (see Schnall et al. 2008). The
same principle applies to tackling an academic challenge: our
perception of the difficulty is "shaped by how much energy
it would take to negotiate the space or situation," explains
Sian Beilock (2015, 225). Specifically, as she explains, "the
cardiac stress reaction that is often created by challenging
mental tests is smaller when you are accompanied by a supportive person than when you are alone." In a collaborative
exercise, students who have built familiar, comfortable,
and trustworthy relationships can encourage each other
so that a difficult task becomes less intimidating. The plea-
sures of learning can likewise be amplified through social
connection, even when that involves simply being present
for an experience together. "Coexperience," as psychologist

Erica J. Boothby and colleagues (2017, 694) coin the term, involves "simply experiencing something in parallel with a close other—without communication or any explicit inter- action," such as looking at images together. When coexpe- riencers share relationship safety, they spend less energy monitoring their social situation, and pay closer attention to the environment. Witnessing stimuli in the company of trusted others made the objects seem more appealing and even more real. "Coexperiencing stimuli with close trusted others may result in less distraction and deeper engagement with the stimuli in one's environment. . . . We speculate that stimuli experienced with close others may benefit dually from deeper processing and commitment to memory on the one hand and greater accessibility for recall on the other" (Boothby et al. 2017, 696, 709). This finding has amazing potential for its application to learning. The phenomenon of coexperience suggests that learning in the company of others with whom we have developed trust and comfort actually improves the depth of our cognitive processing.

Researchers have detected differences in areas of the brain related to processing social stress among urban and rural dwellers. In a series of studies, those with broader social networks (the urban dwellers) were shown through fMRI scans to respond with increased sensitivity to social stress, detectable in the activity of their amygdalae and their perigenual anterior cingulate cortices (see Lederbogen et al. 2011). Increased sensitivity to social stress can produce un- desirable results in the mental health of a large population, but the study also suggests that those with a wider range of social encounters have "busier" brains. Their available models for predicting others' behavior are more numerous and varied, which makes them quick to detect slight signals, and can increase their sense of connection and ability to empathize (see Claxton 2015, 215–16). For college students, interacting productively with a diverse range of others through collaborative work broadens their lived experiences and usefully informs future expectations and interactions. Positive social interactions are good for each of them as individuals and good for the society they affect in turn.

HOW TO GENERATE POSITIVE COLLABORATIVE EXPERIENCES BY INVOLVING THE BODY

Lead Them through Physical Exercises That Build Relationships

The body offers an affordance to promote positive social interactions. Our default mode of social interaction is imitation; the discovery of the mirror neuron system in macaque monkeys in the 1990s has led to intense debate among scientists about the exact nature of this system in humans, and whether we can rightly claim it as an empathy mechanism (see Claxton 2015, 210). In conversation, we might mirror another person's gestures, facial expressions, posture, or movement as a way of creating a sense of shared identity, often without conscious attention. It's one way we indicate to others that we want to establish a connection with them. Our mimicry of facial expressions has been labeled by psychologists as "embodied simulation" that can produce a larger phenomenon known as "emotional contagion" (see Gallese 2004; Hatfield 1993). Studies from recent decades have tested rapid, unconscious mimicry of both positive and negative facial expressions and suggest that "compared to happiness, which has rapid and effortless response, we attend to angry faces with more attention and cognitive resources to figure out and fight against the potential threats"

(Deng and Hu 2018, 7). Our degree of uncertainty about the situation also seems to affect the rapidity of our response. Rapid mimicry and emotional contagion are not only primate phenomena but have been observed between humans and dogs as well, so that stronger social bonds produce higher levels of rapid mimicry (see Palagi et al. 2015). Mimicking a specific facial expression that requires making eye contact can produce a powerful kind of connection.

While the recent work of psychologists confirms embodied, socially shared expressions of emotion, these same observations have been made by poets and artists for centuries, and in the mid-twentieth century by philosophers such as Ludwig Wittgenstein in *Remarks on the Philosophy of Psychology* (1946–49) and Maurice Merleau-Ponty in *Phenomenology of Perception* (1962). Philosopher and embodied cognition researcher Joel Krueger (2009, 683) cites Wittgenstein's (G. E. M. Anscombe translation, 1980) musings on the physical ways that we know others' thoughts: "Look into someone else's face, and see the consciousness in it, and a particular *shade* of consciousness. You see on it, in it, indifference, interest, excitement, torpor, and so on. The light in other people's faces. Do you look into *yourself* in order to recognize the fury in *his* face? It is there as clearly as it is in your own breast." Reviewing philosophical literature on the "extended mind," Krueger argues for the social and moral importance of developing sensitivity to facial signals. Studies done by psychologist Paul Ekman with Zen Buddhist practitioners, for example, reveal their acute sensitivity to "microexpressions":

"Microexpressions" are rapid facial expressions that seem to be common to all cultures. They last "less than one-fifth of a second [and] are one important source of leakage, revealing an

emotion a person is trying to conceal" (Ekman 2003, 15). Because they happen so quickly, they normally operate beneath
the attentional threshold of both the person who has them
and the person who observes them. . . . The Buddhist contem-
platives in Ekman's study scored significantly higher than any
of the other five thousand people Ekman had previously
tested—two standard deviations above the norm—in their
ability to detect microexpressions. They did better than police
officers, lawyers, psychiatrists, customs officials, judges, and
even Secret Service agents. (Krueger 2009, 693–94)

While we may not achieve the level of expertise demonstrated by those with many years of contemplative practice, offering students a chance to observe and respond to
each other's facial expressions is one way to improve their
social connectedness. As an opening exercise for collaborative groups, try asking students to check in with each other
emotionally and nonverbally. The first member of the group
should share a facial expression that communicates their
current mood, to which group members respond by mimicking that face. Each person takes a turn sharing their current
affective state, and others mirror it in return. As Krueger
(2009, 694) suggests, "This bodily skill is the first step in
developing a true ethics of responsiveness." By reflecting
each other's personal expressions, the group can intentionally produce feelings of social connection.

"Interpersonal synchrony" is the phrase used by cognitive
psychologists to describe coordinated movement between
people, which can mean a wide range of behaviors: think of
moving a piece of furniture together with others or playing
a game of catch or dancing to set steps as a couple or with
a group. Even "the wave" practiced by sports fans in stadi-
ums counts as interpersonal synchrony—and produces the

resulting effect of social connection. Scientists have done fascinating studies to explore our instinctive pull toward coordinated and rhythmic motion, building on the Haken-Kelso-Bunz model, the eponymous biomechanical theory that predicts the rate at which bodies fall into or out of synchrony. When participants in a series of experiments were seated in rocking chairs next to each other and asked to rock at individual paces, natural "tuning" factors drew them into a coordinated pattern, "pulled to the rhythm of others through visual or auditory information about the others' movement" (Marsh 2013, 239). A similar phenomenon can happen through walking or even breathing.

This natural inclination of bodies to fall into synchrony and thereby smooth out social interactions suggests another productive approach for collaborative learning. In essence, any activity that gives students a chance to move in coordinated ways can improve their shared sense of identity, and willingness to work toward a collective goal. "Under some circumstances," social psychologist Kerry Marsh (2013, 242) suggests, "it seems that synchrony can be used to overcome the normal behavioral distance between members of different groups." Here are a few activities to use as preparation for better collaborative interactions:

- Ask students to help arrange the furniture for the day's class plan. In addition to giving them a sense of ownership in the classroom space, maneuvering tables and chairs together to achieve a shared vision will stimulate cooperative intentions that cross over into academic collaboration.
- Introduce a name game on the first day of class that involves playing catch. Stand in a circle together (or form several, for a large class). Bring a soft foam ball, and begin by asking each person to clearly say their name before making eye contact

with someone else in the circle and gently tossing the ball to that person. Let the group know they'll need to remember as many names as possible. Once all have stated their names, start the round again, this time requiring them to make eye contact and name someone else before tossing that person the ball. Help with remembering will be fine—the point here is actually to get the students working in interpersonal synchrony, with the side benefit of learning each other's names.

- Use a theater improv variation on the ball-toss exercise as an activity to generate ideas or recall important terms. Instead of stating a name, the first person makes a gesture or body movement, then contributes a word or phrase related to the topic. For example, my Renaissance literature students might be learning the hallmarks of English sonnets. One person might clap hands to associate with iambic pentameter, or another person might make a gesture of hands on heart to associate with "theme of romantic love." The rest of the circle copies each movement and speaks the word or phrase. Once everyone has created their own movement with a relevant word or phrase, the members pass around the movements and associated words. One person starts with their own movement and phrase, then points to another to recall their movement and phrase. Then that person would repeat their movement and phrase and point to someone else, until everyone has had a turn, and all of the generated phrases have been recalled.

- Teach students a simple line dance or series of hand movements as a ritual to begin class or to begin the collaborative activity for that day. Have a large auditorium practice "the wave."

One last word on the use of ritual. Recent findings on the impact of social rituals suggest that ritual mitigates against performance anxiety by relieving uncertainty. Simple rituals that involve the body, like stretching fingers, hands, and arms in deliberate ways while breathing deeply, can help to ground tasks that require executive brain function. Working memory, planning, and prioritizing can be facilitated by "dulling the neural response to performance failure" (Hobson et al. 2017, 19). As Stanford University d.school faculty Kurzat Ozenc and Margaret Hagen (2019, 5) explain, "With more empirical study of rituals, psychologists have discovered that their power derives from their ability to link the physical with the psychological and the emotional." Ozenc and Hagen (2019) offer ritual ideas from psychologists, designers, coaches, behavioral scientists, and others in *Rituals for Work*. This book includes rituals designed to create community, as well as to mitigate conflict and promote resilience. Number 8, "Surrealist Portraits," inspires creative teamwork by directing groups to create collective self-portraits, passed around in four rounds (the ritual aspect) for each person to draw just one-quarter of their own face on a page folded into fourths. The charming results can be displayed in the room or scanned and shared in a course learning site.

Nudge Students to Get Better Sleep

The topic of sleep might well belong anywhere in this book, but its impact on our sociality argues for sleep's critical role in improving collaboration. In his 2017 book *Why We Sleep*, neuroscientist Matthew Walker explains the specific health functions of stages of sleep, both REM (rapid eye movement) and non-REM, and how they contribute to human social interactions. While non-REM sleep performs a necessary "power-cleansing" of the frontal cortex—our center of executive functioning and self-control—it's REM sleep that "exquisitely recalibrates and fine-tunes the emotional circuits of the human brain" and fuels creativity by constructing association networks (Walker 2017, 74). We are not only better able to solve our own tangled problems by giving ourselves ample REM sleep, but we improve our sociality and ability to cooperatively problem-solve with others. Our brains participate in a "fluid, divergent, and 'open-minded' " state of information processing during and after REM sleep (225). Walker speculates that the increase in REM sleep that occurred when early humans began sleeping on the ground "was a key trigger that rocketed Homo sapiens to the top of evolution's lofty pyramid" due to the way it facilitates emotional and social problem-solving (74). The importance of sleep rivals both diet and exercise for maintaining our overall well-being. By supporting positive social interaction in collaborative work, sleep may be the single most important factor in maintaining necessary bandwidth for learning.

The experience of emerita college president and educational researcher Beverly Daniel Tatum transformed her own views on the importance of sleep. After witnessing the powerful difference that prioritizing sleep made for her own well-being, Tatum created the Wellness Revolution at Spelman College in 2012, "a holistic initiative designed to empower and educate Spelman women and the communities they will influence on key components of lifelong wellness— eating better, moving more and sleeping well" (Spelman 2019). Naming this initiative a "revolution" is no exaggeration; the norms of college culture seem to condone abuse of physical well-being, since healthy eating and sleeping habits are perceived as necessary sacrifices to academic dedication. College students regularly pull all-nighters and then brag about going without sleep as a badge of honor. While we can boost students' energy temporarily by bringing shots of glucose (fruit, juices) to class, a longer-term strategy would be to consider structural safeguards:

- Set assignment deadlines before 10 p.m., not midnight, to send an important signal about the value of a full night's sleep; and
- Offer first-year courses you teach no earlier than 9 a.m. to allow students enough time for sleep and a quick breakfast.

As with other pedagogical strategies, transparency about the scientific evidence allows students to buy into the efficacy of paying attention to the body. Experimental results have conclusively documented the ways that sleep loss impairs cognitive performance (Engle-Friedman et al. 2008; Cavanagh 2015). The American Academy of Sleep Medicine offers educational resources online (sleepeducation.org) through the Healthy Sleep Awareness Project, including a short public service announcement video, "Make Time to Sleep," and a bedtime calculator. The "Sleep Well, Be Well" infographic covers healthy sleep habits, and a list of site articles cover sleep disorders. As the University of St. Thomas's Center for College Sleep Scientific Director Roxanne Prichard boils it down for students, "Sleep is your superpower."

Pay Close Attention to Postures and Proximity

Body language is spoken and heard by students working in groups, even when they are not consciously attending to it. Others' postures and proximity, as well as the environment of the space, will affect the quality of the interaction; eye contact facilitates thinking about others' perceptions. At a bare minimum, we can call attention to these matters by taking a few extra seconds to ensure that group members can make solid eye contact with each other (see Khalid et al. 2016), and check that the furniture is not creating an obstacle to productive interaction. Beginning class with the nonverbal, facial "check-in" exercise is one way to give groups a chance to adjust their physical arrangement. We can also allow groups to experience various arrangements for themselves as a way of calling their attention to the difference it makes. Flutist and Licensed Body Mapping Educator Andrée Martin (personal communication 2019) has used this approach effectively by asking music ensembles to stand and repeat a passage or piece normally played while seated:

> When I hear a new student chamber ensemble in a coaching, the first thing I have them do is ask them to act and move as if they are soloists by raising their music stands and getting up off their chairs. The differences in breathing, sound, intonation, clarity of musical intention, and communication with each other and with the audience is instant. While seated, whole body movement can be awkward, stilted, or nonexistent and the energy in the room is low. Students are less likely to get their eyes out of their scores and they tend to rely on one person in the group to lead. The whole body macro and micromovement that happens while standing can help musicians find more expressive possibilities through, in part, imitation of each other's physical gestures.

I have also noticed an improved whole-class discussion by asking everyone to stand around the perimeter of the classroom as we talk. While my students agreed that they are more engaged when standing (and phones are out of reach), they also gradually lost the necessary energy to stand for extended periods later as the term progressed—a palpable demonstration of their energy resources diminishing over a fifteen-week semester.

Another way to call attention to postures, proximity, and behavior within different kinds of spaces is to analyze it in our subject matter. As an activity for an outdoor class session with my Shakespeare class, I considered ways to integrate students' experiences of campus spaces with the experiences of characters and settings in the history play *Henry IV, Part 1*. The task involved exploring how spaces on campus inform our own behavior, and to move and talk with others between locations to form an argument about what Shakespeare does with roles and spaces in the play. For those unfamiliar with *Henry IV, Part 1*, its foregrounding of class structures and unusual mix of both elite and ordinary settings are oft-studied, salient aspects of the play. We could easily have spent the same single period in our classroom, with me lecturing on the text's use of roles and places while they took notes. Integrating an embodied experience with the content material required more imagination, on my part and on the part of the students. But the written insights they produced were more interesting and engaging as a result. One stop for the assignment asked students to survey a large student and faculty parking lot from the hillside; while considering how the parking lot reflects campus power dynamics, they read a passage from the play's final battle scene in which John Falstaff fakes his own death, then claims false credit for killing the formidable warrior Percy Hotspur. Students made insightful observations about how people react to places governed by rules for social behavior, such as Alexander Proft's reflective discussion post: "Falstaff would certainly be the type to park in a faculty spot if he thought he could get away with it/it benefited him, as his actions in Act 5, Scene 4 show us that he reconciles his aversion to the ideal of glory and honor while still making the underhanded effort to obtain it by pretending to have killed Hotspur." As upper-level English majors, my students have had practice making unlikely comparisons and recognizing symbolic or figurative meanings. But recasting Falstaff as an opportunistic parking scofflaw exceeded my expectations for this activity. The students demonstrated a deeper, more personal engagement with the material when given a chance to impose the world of the play on their own familiar environment.

Role-Play

One common practice for facilitating collaborative activities is to assign each member of the group a particular role and task, such as recorder, questioner, or summarizer. While assigning roles does ensure a smoother completion of the task at hand, it relieves the group of a critical but messy step in collaborative work: identifying and choosing appropriate functions for each member. Very rarely do authentic tasks and problems that benefit from social collaboration come with scripted roles for each person to follow. It's well worth the buy-in from students to spend time having groups identify what functions may be needed to perform a task effectively, what specific demands or skills will be needed to perform these functions, and how to equitably distribute the work. We can build transparency into collaboration by offering a structured process for approaching goals, tasks, and timelines, rather than skipping over that step and prescribing these ourselves. Allowing them to check in along the way and reflect on their experiences develops their understanding of these skills. As they develop greater self-awareness (and, ideally, empathy for others), students might consider the following questions relevant to embodied cognition:

- How did your affective state—the mood produced by your body's available energy and other demands on your attention—impact your participation?
- How might past experiences have shaped your expectations of others' attitudes and behavior in this setting?

Spending time to learn a process for approaching collaboration may help to save time in the long run, because students can own and monitor the assigned roles they've set for themselves. We might also provide formal guidelines that describe ways to facilitate the contributions of others, such as the American Association of Colleges and Universities' VALUE Rubric for Teamwork, available online.

Self-assigning functional roles helps students to develop a specific set of collaborative skills; enacting wholly artificial or fictional roles with a group "wakes up" the brain by disrupting its ability to smoothly predict others' behavior. Role-playing pedagogies like *Reacting to the Past* games or in-class debates with assigned sides are effective for many reasons relevant to embodiment: there is standing and movement during the activity, and the unscripted nature of the interaction allows learning to take place through play. As historian Mark Carnes (2014, 112, 123), founder of the *Reacting* pedagogy, explains in his book about developing and implementing educational role-playing games, "These [historical] characters appeal precisely because they are so different. They taunt our metaself for being predictable, for adhering to social hierarchies and conventions. They evoke absurd and outrageous alternatives. . . . When we identify with other people, whether by reading novels, watching

Fig. 5.1. Students moving freely around the classroom while involved in a role-playing game at University of Wisconsin–LaCrosse. (Photograph by James Longhurst, 2019. Used by permission.)

plays, or engaging in role-immersion games, we enlarge our cognitive universe. We gain access to more information and new ideas. But something else occurs, too. We find strangers less strange."

Role-playing allows students to expand their brains' repertoire of expectations, since not only do they meet new kinds of people as characters, they temporarily inhabit a new kind of person's worldview—sometimes a person whose experiences and views differ quite markedly from their own. Role-playing simultaneously taps into the cognitive benefit of moving around together during class.

Role-playing games that engage the body are often fun, and funny. And making learning fun can go a long way toward overcoming a series of bad experiences with collaborative work, for both teachers and students. Acknowledging and engaging students as social beings can enhance their motivation and ability to learn. As clinical psychiatrist Daniel J. Siegel (2006, xv–xvi) describes the social nature of embodied brains, "The brain is hard-wired to connect to other minds, to create images of others' intentional states, affective expressions, and bodily states of arousal that, through our mirror neuron system's fundamental capacity to create emotional resonance, serve as the gateway to empathy. In this way, the mind is both relational and embodied." The practice we give our students with forming empathic relationships matters to their success as human beings. Collaborative work is both exceptionally complex and fundamentally meaningful. Learning to work productively with diverse others does lead to better ideas and outcomes, but it also enhances our mutual enjoyment of learning and spreads outward to affect social interactions more broadly in the world.

Chapter Six

. . . .

EMBRACE DISCOMFORT

. . . .

In arguing for the centrality of the body to learning, a stance supported by contemporary neuroscience, I've made these specific recommendations for teachers:

1. Recognize the impact of our physical spaces on learning;
2. Take our classes outside whenever we can;
3. Infuse learning with sensory experiences;
4. Build movement into our classroom time; and
5. Use movement to build social relationships among students.

Some of these actions require only a shift in attitude and awareness on the part of faculty, a shift that costs no money and requires little investment of institutional resources. But this attitudinal change will mean swimming against the current of educational and cultural norms. The nature of academic work is sedentary, and our working habits align with recent U.S. trends showing that sitting time increased between 2007 and 2016 (Yang et al. 2019). The importance of physical health to the optimal functioning of brains remains underrecognized, hindered by our long heritage of Cartesian body/mind duality.

Embracing discomfort applies first to us as faculty. We gained entry into the professoriate because we were able and willing to dedicate years of our lives to reading in chairs and sofas and beds, writing at desks, and generally spending our days indoors in labs or studios or behind computer screens. The present reward for our labors might involve the "perks" of having offices close to classrooms, parking spaces close to buildings: entitlements that allow us to exert the least possible physical energy while at work. This system has not been kind to our health. In a remarkable blog post, "Treadmill Desk: A Testimonial," neuroscientist Daniel Bor (2015) describes his own transformation after adopting a practice of standing and walking while at work:

> I wish I'd implemented a treadmill desk 20 years ago. And I definitely plan to carry on with this habit for the rest of my life, not just for the health reasons, but because I can work so much more effectively while being physically active. Spending my office time walking has protected me from illness, and improved my weight and stamina. It has radically aided my quality of sleep. And my alertness and focus at work has significantly increased. . . . I also think it's time we evaluate optimal systems for schools, universities, seminars, conferences, office-based businesses and so on. For concentration, productivity and health, perhaps the default during the day should be to stand.

Bor's testimony may be echoed by others whose daily habits have improved during the 2020 pandemic work-from-home mandate, spending more time outside on walks, for instance. Now that we've been forced to learn how much our individual and communal well-being matters, we ought to apply to our own daily habits what science shows we need for optimal functioning: solid rest, nutritious food, and plenty of movement—outside, when possible—throughout the day. We can develop a practice of paying attention to our bodies' internal sensations, our proximal environments, and our corresponding mood and level of concentration to optimize our cognitive performance. Just as sharing with students that we ourselves have struggled as learners, we can share with them our own evolving journeys toward body/mind health.

Once we've embraced our own discomforts, we can lead the way for students. Faculty across the country are pursuing what we might call a pedagogy of discomfort with impressive results. At Northeastern University, Khoury School of Computer Science students are taken out of their comfort zones through theater improv games; classes practice making eye contact, stretching to stand up straight, speaking in gibberish, and power-posing. The end goal is to produce more natural public speakers and better collaborators, and these goals are achieved through a heightened body awareness and a sense of belonging that comes from doing "absurd" things together. President Joseph Aoun sees the course as a means to "sharpen uniquely human skills" (Castellanos 2019). CASE U.S. Professor of the Year for 2008 and Kansas State anthropologist Michael Wesch uses as assignment called "Get Uncomfortable" as one of ten challenges in his 101-level Anthropology for Everyone class. These challenges are designed specifically to push students and to have them carefully reflect on their own experience of being uncomfortable. Confronting new or unfamiliar situations "immediately opens your mind," according to a student testimonial on the course YouTube site (Wesch 2018), and left her "super awakened," which is exactly the result we would expect from short-circuiting the embodied brain's default prediction mode.

We can further embrace discomfort by starting conversations with colleagues about how to develop and articulate informed institutional philosophies about the integral relationship between bodies and minds. These will be hard conversations. The current discourse around student bodies in higher ed has mostly to do with protecting bodies from harm and respecting their diversity, both imperative needs. Talking about bodies and bodily health will demand the utmost empathy, because perspectives differ widely, and our bodies are the most intensely personal aspect of experiences and identities. My experience of writing this book and anticipating readers' reactions makes me all too aware that messages about health, ability, and well-being can be heard as "body shaming." One recent op-ed in a national magazine objected to "food-shaming" by co-workers as an indirect means to criticize bodies. These are regrettable developments, and I think concepts like "wellness" and "body shaming" can indeed become code language for oversimplifying and categorizing a diverse and complex range of lived experiences. We are going to have to talk more openly about our own experiences of embodiment in order to find our way to more nuanced and informed positions. Roxane Gay's book *Hunger* (2017) and C. S. Giscombe's "The Amputee Cyclist's Art of Self-Repair" (2019) are important contributions to this conversation, sharing and interrogating particular experiences of embodiment.

As it stands, our underexamined attitudes toward the body discount routine physical health as a priority for most faculty and students. The experiences of student athletes might serve as interesting case studies for integrating physical and cognitive performance that can influence wider campus culture. Coaches have specific knowledge and experiences that faculty might learn from to develop body-aware, cognitive performance skills. Brown University's Sheridan Center for Teaching and Learning has developed a learning community for faculty and coaches, one excellent model for beginning to bridge the academic-athletic divide. The typical segregation between academic affairs and athletic departments, however, makes these connections rare and potentially tricky to navigate. Coaches may also need faculty to raise their awareness of how training or travel schedules are affecting student athletes' cognitive performance. The embodied brains of our student athletes merit special consideration, and the vulnerability of low-socioeconomic scholarship players and the risk of head trauma in certain sports make this especially worth examining.

There are older positions on body/mind integration we might ponder. In 1904 the last will of British imperialist Cecil J. Rhodes—once himself a sickly child—established an expectation for Rhodes Scholarship candidates to demonstrate physical vigor, still expressed in the criteria for the award as "energy to use one's talents to the full (as demonstrated by mastery in areas such as sports, music, debate, dance, theatre, and artistic pursuits, particularly where teamwork is involved)" (Rhodes Trust 2019). While Rhodes's colonialist legacy has generated plenty of controversy at Oxford, his privileging of physical stamina strikes me as an astute priority, albeit for wrong-headed reasons. Rhodes considered an interest and skill in sports to be an essential quality of manliness, and the Rhodes Trust's revision of the selection criteria in 2018 shows wisdom in its careful use of language. "Energy to use one's talents" does not exclude candidates with physical disabilities but recognizes that vitality plays an important role in academic achievement. Rhodes Scholar Pasquale Toscano has argued persuasively that the inherent challenges of moving through the world with a physical disability requires increased bandwidth to navigate stressors that are nonexistent for the nondisabled. Living with a disability, Toscano (2017) writes, can be an "epistemologically enriching experience" that motivates him to want to share these insights through his own work. Toscano's own experience of intense physical therapy after spinal cord injury effectively exemplifies the kind of bodily energy necessary to pursue ambitious intellectual goals. Wellness and disability are not mutually exclusive categories, and we must be willing to embrace discomfort in developing inclusive practices and policies that recognize cognitive processes as inextricably embodied.

BEYOND DESCARTES

It's time to learn from Descartes by viewing his position with a compassionate eye. Having recognized that our physical senses can be deceived and therefore may not accurately represent reality, he sought refuge in cognition: *cogito ergo sum*. Despite that motto's seeming confidence in the brain, Descartes knew that cognition (or human reasoning) was fallible, too. He was determined to find and establish orderly, mathematical principles for reasoning. I want to give him credit for identifying the truly uncomfortable nature of being human: we can't count on either our bodies or our minds to accurately represent reality. Descartes wanted to be able to overcome our faulty perceptions of the world, but his only tool—the brain—was one source of the problem. The insights of cognitive psychology and neuroscience now offer us another way to consider the situation. We're learning about specific ways the human brain has evolved that shape its cognitive biases. I think Descartes would be thrilled to know that cognitive biases are empirically provable through rigorous experimental methods and the technology of functional MRI imaging. He would also be right if he perceived the alarming and urgent need for humanity to quickly share and apply what we know: our continued existence may depend on it.

Cognitive biases have provided the basis for some of the most fascinating and popular nonfiction books of recent years: Stephen J. Dubner and Steven Levitt's *Freakonomics* (2005), Malcolm Gladwell's *Blink* (2005), Daniel Kahneman's *Thinking, Fast and Slow* (2011), and Hans Rosling's *Factfulness* (2018). The authors of these books provide evidence, examples, and anecdotes to help readers understand how the processes of our own thinking are prone to certain kinds of errors that can cause us to be our own worst enemies. We are not objectively rational perceivers of reality but creatures of planet earth whose behaviors have evolved over millions of years in response to specific conditions—like any other animal species. The book in your hands now pursues the same project by encouraging readers to change the conditions of human schooling to be more in tune with evolutionary, embodied cognitive processes.

If we took a Cartesian approach to cognitive biases, we might consider developing formulas for identifying and remedying each prospective ill. Confirmation bias, *check*. Group attribution error, *check*. Rosling's *Factfulness* provides a list of ten rules of thumb as a checklist to guard against our instincts, including "Straight Line" (relying on experience to predict the future). Rosling defines critical thinking as the ability to change your mind and stay open to new ideas. Yet there are far more than ten biases to overcome; one beautiful infographic organizes 188 cognitive biases into a terrifying wheel of irrationality (Desjardins 2017). If the idea of checking our every impulse against a bias calculator feels a bit demoralizing, I suggest we might simply follow Socrates's dictate: Know Thyself. The best approach to unavoidable human error is to remain uncertain and curious about one's own perceptions and behavior and to seek self-awareness and growth through a heightened attention to one's embeddedness within a dynamic ecosystem. It's a great long-term project, since the self is a moving, shape-shifting target. And it demands vital bodily energy.

The science of embodied cognition supports the value of a growth mindset, and of curiosity as a primary means of lifelong well-being. That means putting ourselves in unfamiliar positions and remaining open to ideas that may be unpleasant or even threatening. Cultivating a habit of curiosity means not only resisting the paths of familiar experience during young adulthood but continuing to do so as we age. At age seventy, Fred "Mister" Rogers was profiled in *Esquire* magazine, interviewed stark naked as he undressed for his daily swim; as writer Tom Junod (2017) recalls, "There was an energy to him . . . a fearlessness, an unashamed insistence on intimacy, and though I tried to ask him questions about himself, he always turned the questions back on me." Here was a literally naked human being, facing a reporter whose sole focus was learning more about his subject, but the reporter found most compelling the subject's own unselfconscious, unshakable curiosity. Becoming the "architect of your own experience," in Lisa Feldman Barrett's words, demands a high degree of curiosity and self-awareness: body awareness, emotional awareness, and social awareness, which we should address explicitly in the classroom. Mindfulness exercises, narrative reflections on personal growth, and meaningful shared experiences allow us to examine and even embrace discomfort, with the goal of shaping not only our own minds, but the wider cultural mind.

Pursuing growth and self-knowledge means embracing discomfort through resisting our ingrained, prediction-based habits of perception. Developing a habit of questioning our own perceptions can help us to develop self-compassion as well as empathy for others. Studies have shown that engaging in regular practices of expressing compassion, gratitude, and pride increases our ability to value the future, an especially important but difficult task for humans. (Procrastination, for example, might be best understood as an undervaluing or lack of compassion for our future selves.) Psychologist David Desteno (2017) summarizes the results of over a decade's work on this subject by his lab: "Feeling pride or compassion has been shown to increase perseverance on difficult tasks by over 30 percent. Likewise, gratitude and compassion have been tied to better academic performance, a greater willingness to exercise and eat healthily, and lower levels of consumerism, impulsivity and tobacco and alcohol use. If using willpower causes stress, using these emotions actually heals: They slow heart rate, lower blood pressure and reduce feelings of anxiety and depression. By making us value the future more, they ease the way to patience and perseverance." These are significant findings for directly impacting academic performance and recovering students' necessary bandwidth for learning. How might we tie into coursework expressions of pride, gratitude, and compassion? These expressions follow naturally when human beings make things with their own hands and use their bodies for work. Behavioral economists have labeled this cognitive bias the "IKEA effect"; creating something with our own hands allows us to demonstrate our competency and thus place more value on things we've built ourselves (see Norton et al. 2012).

MAKING THINGS, USING OUR BODIES, AND FACING WICKED PROBLEMS

The work of anthropologist Ellen Dissanayake shows that creating physical objects—those we might call tools as well as those we might call art—developed as evolutionary traits of humans. In her book *Art and Intimacy* (2000), Dissanayake argues that humans are born with a capacity and need for mutuality: belonging to a social group, finding and making meaning, acquiring a sense of competence through handling and making, and elaborating meanings and competencies as a way of expressing their importance. While some evolutionary traits, like our built-in cognitive biases, have become maladaptive in modern society, "other predispositions—making things with our hands, using our bodies for work—have atrophied through disuse and disinclination" (13). As she defines it, art is a behavior that is interactive, hands on, emotionally rewarding and psychologically meaningful, communal, and supportive of identity (184–85). Dissanayake's generous and broadly understood definition of art encompasses many behaviors we don't normally identify this way: dressing ourselves, curating our social media presence, or hosting parties. Planning and implementing a learning experience—the art of teaching, I'd argue—falls squarely into this framework. Including the opportunity for students to create tangible products or embodied performances builds new strength into these human predispositions. Producing tangible results that are shared with a public audience, one of the essential elements of a high-impact practice as defined by George Kuh and Carol Geary Schneider (2008), elicits moments of compassion, gratitude, and pride.

Humans' efforts to assimilate new knowledge and experiences provide our brains with genuine pleasure. Pleasurable feelings accompany a relative ease of cognitive assimilation—ease is "both a cause and a consequence of a pleasant feeling," according to Daniel Kahneman (2011, 69)—and depend on being able to bring the required amount of bodily energy to the task. The first mode of learning, which I've referred to earlier as *noticing*, we might also consider in terms of pleasure as *savoring*. Attending closely to objects, landscapes, words, and images offers our embodied brains the opportunity to notice distinctive features. Savoring builds on noticing by adding self-awareness to the process; the Chinese notion of savoring called *p'in wei* includes attending, grasping context, letting one's imagination go, and being aware of one's feelings (see Fridja and Sundararajan 2007). I know it's hard to savor something unless I slow down and permit myself to indulge in paying attention to my surroundings. Noticing and savoring require that we carefully arrange our learning environment and that we make use of students' sensory perceptions while allowing them to move. Savoring also requires building in moments for reflection.

Imitating, as a second mode of learning, offers the potential not only for pleasure, but for healing. For disciplines like music performance, or lab sciences that require precise finger dexterity, or writing and coding fields that demand a lot of computer keyboarding, teaching students to develop a heightened body awareness can prevent and heal repetitive motion injuries. Music educator Bonnie Draina attributes a loss of body awareness to years of traditional schooling, when we're made to sit still and focus on external stimuli: "We teach ourselves to 'turn off' or ignore our kinesthetic sense. . . . All of that leads to the exclusion of kinesthetic sensory information (which is interoceptive—about us) and a disconnect from our body. Once we are no longer kinesthetically aware, when we stop taking in that information about our physical movement, the brain is less able to modify our body maps as our bodies change" (qtd. in Eady 2019). Draina recommends reversing this loss of kinesthetic awareness by guiding students to develop interoceptive and proprioceptive sensitivity. Increasing body awareness can involve asking them to notice and imitate others' movements. That might involve experimenting with a series of different postures, for example, and noticing how each affects our own internal response, as well as communicates a message to others. In his TEDx Talk, "How Your Movements Can Heal Your Brain," Neuroplastic Training Institute of Toronto director Joaquin Farias (2015, 5:20–35) describes the role of imitation in re-habilitating movement: "When the neuro software is not accessible in the brain, you can transfer it by mimicking another person's movements and make them yours. When your brain accepts the transfer, a neuro-plastic change will start. It's a reorganization of the whole brain." Imitation is the body's route to deep learning. As we learn new patterns of interoceptive, exteroceptive, and proprioceptive perception, our sense of consciousness itself transforms.

If the transformation of consciousness seems rather ambitious as a goal for higher education, the nature of contemporary problems may necessitate it. Our common well-being—our survival—depends on people working better together. We are facing a number of so-called wicked problems (see Rittell and Webber 1973): complex, continually evolving problems that resist clear definition, so that the necessary conditions for designing "correct" solutions evade our grasp. Wicked problems are rooted in causes viewed differently by different stakeholders and cannot be solved by any single action or decision. The complexity of wicked problems, like immune-resistant viruses and terrorism, often results in solutions that spawn new wicked problems. Because of the additional urgent need for action, some public policy experts have deemed the consequences created by climate change a "super wicked" problem. The cognitive vulnerabilities of humans make it especially difficult to analyze the root causes of complex issues and work toward future solutions.

Facing wicked problems depends on our awareness of human cognitive vulnerabilities, and of the ways our interactions are informed by instinctive responses that may not be constructive. Our evolutionary instincts to seek certainty and assign blame, for example, have provided the foundation for a system of law that overrelies on witness identification. Neuroscientists and justice reform advocates have called for reexamining this practice, as well as our standard practices for bench trial and trial by jury, because both are easily compromised by human factors like a decision's closeness to lunch. The cognitive vulnerability of humans likewise informs emerging artificial intelligence technologies. The development of deep-fake news, for example, builds models of human voices and bodies to simulate behavior that appears authentic. We are gullible because of our propensity to rely on past experience to inform perception, rather than exert energy to notice revealing details. To minimize these weaknesses and capitalize on our strengths, we need to help learners develop self-awareness about human cognitive biases and reinvigorate our uniquely human physical capacities for creating tangible products and performances. Solving wicked problems demands deploying unorthodox strategies.

STRUCTURAL CHANGE IN HIGHER EDUCATION: FOR CAMPUS CHANGE-MAKERS

In advocating for a radical change in the kinds of learning activities we pursue, I don't want to avoid discussing structural changes that do cost money and time. Cathy N. Davidson does not overstate the case when she uses the word "revolutionize" to describe a necessary overhaul for higher education. Moving students away from an industrial model that involves sitting still and listening as primary modes of learning will mean revamping classroom spaces and time. Not only must classroom furniture be mobile, but rooms must be large enough to accommodate movement and circulation for all participants. That can mean lowering the person-capacity of existing rooms by about 30 percent. It might argue for the end of large lecture halls, or at least decreasing their number. While it has been possible for some faculty with more than one hundred students to incorporate active learning strategies, it's clearly time to reconsider whether such large class sizes reflect an outdated factory-model view of education. If there's a cognitive benefit to be gained from gathering people in large numbers (for example, to share the experience of emotional contagion generated by a crowd), that would seem to argue for its infrequent and special use. Spaces are so critical to human perception and cognition that faculty need to reverse outright the process of being assigned a room for teaching and make intentional choices about which kinds of spaces (including outdoors and off-campus) best suit the learning activities we facilitate. We know that variety is the key to producing more open, attentive states for learning, but classes are structured as standard meetings in the same place, at the same time, for weeks and months and years on end. This structure undermines our very purpose.

Holding in-person classes in a variety of times and locations represents an enormous logistical challenge. It may only be possible as a series of small steps: sticking with uniform meeting days and times but getting out of the classroom more often, for example. Or perhaps it could mean pushing for more mini-terms designed for a single course experience or for more blended or hybrid modes of online and in-person learning. The standard credit-hour and definition of learning by hours of "seat time" (ugh!) rests on an outmoded, factory-model presumption. A five-month-long term with rare interruptions is unforgiving, particularly for students and faculty whose lives outside of school make perfect attendance nearly impossible, and could even be considered inhumane, since it makes little allowance for rest, recovery, or reflection needed for long-term development. It seems increasingly clear that for undergraduate students enrolled in non-selective institutions (in other words, most college students) a degree has represented passage of an endurance test: they were able to complete a long-term commitment. That simple indicator has been useful in the past as a discriminator for employers and correlates with the statistics that show college graduates are good with other long-term projects, like maintaining health and family relationships. But this expectation has also proven to work against the completion of a college degree by students from low-socioeconomic-status backgrounds, who have more fragile support systems and more frequent demands on their time and energy over the course of months and years. Greater flexibility in schedules not only respects the investment of students' time and money in seeking higher education but acknowledges that humans are not machines.

We're already seeing change to the industrial model of measuring learning in the rise of competency-based education and in the design of outcomes-based syllabi. Online learning has changed the game by throwing out the requirement of in-class seat time, and that single factor has instigated a healthy debate among faculty about how we recognize and measure effective teaching and learning in various modes of delivery.

Many of these conversations center on ways to shorten students' time to degree completion or increase efficiency for both the learner and the teacher, a positive outcome if we're looking carefully at excessive demands on time that seem to produce few benefits for learning. But I think we're also at the beginning of trying to measure learning differently, and we'll need to ask important questions about what it really means to undergo a transformative experience—if that's an agreed-upon goal of higher education. Perhaps transformation is an overarching goal that incorporates the mastery of complex knowledge, or the demonstration of advanced skills, or the ability to discover, design, and deliver solutions to ill-defined problems. But that may not happen in one term, or even in four or six years. What if evidence of cognitive transformation isn't really measurable until decades after graduation? Is the norm of a four-year degree earned at age twenty-two really well-suited for transformative learning? The years between ages eighteen and twenty-six are important years for brain maturation, and higher education has benefited from riding on a tailwind of growth that's largely inevitable. In raising the bar to expect cognitive transformation, can we balance the convenient maturation of the adolescent human brain with a longer-term vision?

Our industrial model treats formal education as an inoculation, a vaccine against ignorance that we provide for young adults and then send them on their way for the remaining four, five, six-plus decades of their lives. Education-as-inoculation runs counter to what we now know about neuroplasticity and about the value of curiosity for continual human growth and fulfillment. It's also a bad economic model. The demographic ebb and flow of traditional-aged college students and shifts in their geographical locations continues to wreak havoc on the lives of faculty, staff, and students whose institutions are forced to confront rapid change. Colleges and universities in the United States expanded and multiplied to educate eighteen- to twenty-four-year-olds in the postwar era. Why aren't we reconsidering the structure of higher education to bring the rest of the adult population back to learning? The standard 120-plus-credit-hour undergraduate degree model seems ripe for breaking apart. Outcomes-driven credentials can be earned in shorter bursts with flexible timeframes, and an emerging norm might be the expectation that these opportunities extend throughout a person's lifetime.

Rather than viewing "re"-training and "re"-education as a tragic last resort for those left behind when industries move away or become automated, making the structure of higher learning more permeable could mean that labor forces continually retool themselves. Worker-driven interests could become a dynamic part of economic development. Focused areas driven by local interest might also draw smaller class sizes and better-designed learning experiences. Institutions of higher education must become more agile in meeting the economic needs of communities and the growth interests of society on the whole. And as a disciplinary expert in the humanities, I want to be explicitly clear that I am not advocating for an exclusively vocational model. Developing sensitivity to language, to shifting historical narratives, and to the role of the arts in making human lives meaningful will be absolutely critical in a lifelong learning curriculum. Adult learners will demand education in the arts and humanities because they fulfill essential human wants and needs.

Faculty will need to anticipate these demands by getting out of our disciplinary silos. As disciplines have been categorized and subcategorized over the past century-plus, increasing specialization has come at the expense of understanding messy, complex phenomena. The major purpose served by disciplinary specialization is replication of the existing structure; while deep expertise is certainly valuable, we have become enamored with specialized knowledge and have undervalued the real need to connect and integrate our expertise. As arts education expert Ken Robinson argues in the 2015 documentary film *Most Likely to Succeed* (1:24:39–25:02), a standardized, discipline-based system often falls short in addressing authentic human needs: "Education is a complex human system. It's about people. And people are natural creatures, we're organic creatures. You know, we grow, and we evolve, and we change, and if you have an industrial metaphor in your head, then you're led into the sort of language that we now use about standardization, and the thing is, it's much more like gardening than engineering." Gardening is an apt metaphor for education because it acknowledges our role in the ecosystem of the natural world. Many of the most exciting education initiatives under development now affirm interdisciplinary perspectives by promoting complex learning ecosystems: STEAM (science, technology, engineering, arts, and mathematics), digital humanities, teaching and learning research. At Columbus State University, my own regional public institution, faculty collaborate across departments and colleges to create once-in-a-lifetime learning opportunities for students; the final products of student-faculty interdisciplinary work include performances, exhibitions, research studies, community projects, and tools for K–12 learning. Teams showcase projects at regional and national conferences, extending these transformative experiences through travel. None of this happens, however, without incentives and structural support that institutions must provide and value.

A LEARNING ECOSYSTEM
....

I began this book by introducing six principles of embodied cognition, the last of which is that our bodies reward
learning. We know that brains are deeply embodied, that
bodies are deeply interconnected, and that an ecosystemic
model—not an assembly line—best represents the dynamic
interplay that produces human learning. We're at a turning
point in the business of higher learning, affected by global
and local forces that threaten the survival of many institutions, and I think this threat presents our best opportunity
to transform our approaches to teaching. The technological innovations that have changed our landscape in recent
decades have revealed what *isn't* easily replicated through
online interactions: physical human contact, shared social
experiences, the need to use our bodies to make physical
objects or to perform as a meaningful expression of new
understanding. Students aren't brains on sticks, and if we
ignore the vital role of the body in cognitive perception, we
miss out on enormous potential for deeper learning. Because
the body is always implicated in perception, the health and
physical well-being of student and faculty bodies must be
recognized as an academic issue as well. The evidence for
this imperative, fundamentally grounded in neuroscience
(see Opel et al. 2019), is supported by a wide and eclectic
variety of sources. Popular lifestyle magazines, online news,
and social media sites now regularly explore issues related to
body/mind interconnection, and educational practices have
been slow to integrate these insights.

As I write, the worldwide COVID-19 pandemic has required closing campus classrooms to restrict human interaction; it remains to be seen how this change will impact
higher education in the long term. If our temporary reliance

on screens to create human connection can meet our needs or at least facilitate an education we're prepared to accept as satisfactory, we may do so at the risk of exacerbating the sedentary habits that have been so detrimental to human health and well-being. But I suspect that the current crisis may help to reveal how much we value embodied presence. Online education has the potential to largely free us from "seat time" by using technology more intentionally (see Bruff 2019), by sending students out into the world for learning experiences, and by gathering in person for experiences that are important to share. The confluence of new forces in many areas of human endeavor suggests that change is already underway. The wicked problems of the world are calling for humans' most profound ability to see ourselves as more than the sum of our parts: embodied creatures inextricably connected to each other and to the dynamic, living planet through which we move.

ACKNOWLEDGMENTS

....

This project began in 2016 over pints at the Anchor in Oxford, England, with my brilliant friend and study abroad partner, musician Andrée Martin. I am indebted to Andrée for generously sharing her expertise in the fields of body mapping and embodied cognition. I gained precious time to begin reading and writing at the Bodleian Library, thanks to supportive leadership at Columbus State University (Tina Butcher, Tom Hackett, Chris Markwood) for granting my request to serve as site director at the university's Spencer House in Oxford. The CSU Women's Research and Writing Group provided an important opportunity to draft this book's introduction at a self-funded Florida beach retreat (thanks Amanda Rees, Kimberly Shaw, Cindy Ticknor, Stephanie DaSilva). I am grateful to my CSU English department colleagues and our champion, chair Judi Livingston, for an esprit de corps that fosters great teaching and important scholarly work. Brenda Ivey, Jessica Cook, Courtney Fields, and Stephanie Gutierrez, wonderful staff in the CSU Faculty Center for the Enhancement of Teaching and Learning, provided daily doses of moral support.

The book's focus went through several earlier iterations until Jim Lang and Derek Krissoff at West Virginia

University Press expressed a willingness to patiently work with me on shaping it into something more than three people might want to read. Thank you so much for taking this chance. I am grateful to Cia Verschelden at Malcolm X College, Catie Nielson at Northeastern University, and generous peer reviewers for reading and responding to versions of the manuscript, as well as expert copyeditor Sarah C. Smith. The support and encouragement of fellow authors in the Teaching and Learning in Higher Education Series has been phenomenal and unexpected; you're the best, Squad.

This project has benefited immensely from the generosity of fellow researchers and practitioners who shared their time and expertise with me: Joe Adkins and Jim Kovach of the architecture firm VMDO, Leslie Bayers and Lott Hill at the University of the Pacific, and Bonnie Smith Whitehouse at Belmont University. The University System of Georgia's Center for Teaching and Learning directors' consortium provides a continual font of resources and camaraderie.

I am very fortunate to have been raised by a former collegiate cross-country runner (and all-round sports enthusiast) and a nature-loving outdoorswoman, whose influences here are evident, and whose support for this project has been constant. Thanks, Frank and Marilyn Hrach. My brother and sister-friend, Steve and April, have cheered me throughout the journey, along with aunts Marilyn Kusniss and Joanne Giovannini. I'm proud to be part of the Speck family, in which writing a book is cool, but not as important as being kind. And I'm lucky to be surrounded by friends who provide encouragement and inspiration from their own achievements: looking forward to experiencing social closeness again!

Most of this book was composed on weekend mornings in a small corner room with a green, leafy view of the backyard.

Carolina Dog snoozed helpfully nearby; my partner, poet and teacher Nick Norwood, brewed the coffee and read every word of the developing draft. I would not have had the courage to write a book without witnessing Nick's own daily discipline as a writer or without the seriousness with which he has taken me and my ideas. Thank you for the conversations, the cooking, the cocktails, and the much-needed getaways that made the process of writing a book totally rewarding. Finally, thanks to our brood of grown children—Luke Georgecink, Sarah Georgecink, Sam Georgecink, Graham Norwood, and Natalee Norwood—who provide delightful distractions and tolerate my advice for life's trials: more yoga, more vegetables.

REFERENCES

. . . .

Abrahamson, Dor. 2009. "Embodied Design: Constructing Means for
    Constructing Meaning." *Educational Studies in Mathematics* 70 (1): 27–47.
Anderson, Michael L. 2014. *After Phrenology: Neural Reuse and the Interactive
    Brain.* Cambridge, MA: Bradford.
Barkley, Elizabeth F. 2010. *Student Engagement Techniques: A Handbook for
    College Faculty.* San Francisco: Jossey-Bass.
Barkley, Elizabeth F., Claire Howell Major, and K. Patricia Cross. 2014.
    Collaborative Learning Techniques: A Handbook for College Faculty. 2nd ed.
    The Jossey-Bass Higher and Adult Education Series Collaborative Learning
    Techniques. San Francisco: Jossey-Bass.
Barrett, Lisa Feldman. 2016. "Are You in Despair? That's Good." Gray Matter:
    Science and Society column. *New York Times.* June 3, 2016. https://www
    .nytimes.com/2016/06/05/opinion/sunday/are-you-in-despair-thats-good
    .html.
————. 2017a. *How Emotions Are Made: The Secret Life of the Brain.* New York:
    Houghton Mifflin Harcourt.
————. 2017b. "You Aren't at the Mercy of Your Emotions—Your Brain
    Creates Them." Filmed December 2017 in San Francisco. TED@IBM video,
    18:21. https://www.ted.com/talks/lisa_feldman_barrett_you_aren_t
    _at_the_mercy_of_your_emotions_your_brain_creates_them.
Bayers, Leslie, and Lott Hill. 2019. "Micro-Contemplative Interventions."
    *The Mindful Moment: A Quarterly Newsletter of the Mindfulness and
    Contemplative Pedagogy Special Interest Group of the POD Network.* January
    2019. https://mailchi.mp/4a44099cd1d7/mindful-moment-newsletter
    -1272367.
Beatley, Tim. 2012. "Exploring the Nature Pyramid." *The Nature of Cities.*
    August 7, 2012. https://www.thenatureofcities.com/2012/08/07/exploring
    -the-nature-pyramid/.
Beilock, Sian. 2015. *How the Body Knows Its Mind: The Surprising Power of the*

Physical Environment to Influence How You Think and Feel. New York: Atria Books.

Beilock, Sian L., and Lauren E. Holt. 2007. "Embodied Preference Judgments: Can Likeability Be Driven by the Motor System?" *Psychological Science* 18 (1): 51–57.

Berrett, Dan, and Beckie Supiano. 2019. "One Way to Take the Sting Out of Student Feedback." Teaching Newsletter, *Chronicle of Higher Education*. March 14, 2019. https://www.chronicle.com/article/One-Way-to-Take -the-Sting-Out/245892.

Biederman, Irving, and Edward A. Vessel. 2006. "Perceptual Pleasure and the Brain: A Novel Theory Explains Why the Brain Craves Information and Seeks It through the Senses." *American Scientist* 94 (3): 247–53.

Bischoff-Grethe, Amanda, Megan Martin, Hui Mao, and Gregory S. Berns. 2001. "The Context of Uncertainty Modulates the Subcortical Response to Predictability." *Journal of Cognitive Neuroscience* 13 (7): 986–93.

Blakeslee, Matthew, and Sandra Blakeslee. 2007. *The Body Has a Mind of Its Own: How Body Maps in Your Brain Help You Do (Almost) Everything Better*. New York: Random House.

Boothby, Erica J., Leigh K. Smith, Margaret S. Clark, and John A. Bargh. 2017. "The World Looks Better Together: How Close Others Enhance Our Visual Experiences." *Personal Relationships* 24 (3): 694–714. https://doi.org/10 .1111/pere.12201.

Bor, Daniel. 2015. "Treadmill Desk: A Testimonial." Daniel Bor (blog). July 10, 2015. http://www.danielbor.com/treadmill-desk-a-testimonial/.

Bornemann, Boris, Beate M. Herbert, Wolf E. Mehling, and Tania Singer. 2015. "Differential Changes in Self-Reported Aspects of Interoceptive Awareness through 3 Months of Contemplative Training." *Frontiers in Psychology* 5: 1504. https://doi.org/10.3389/fpsyg.2014.01504.

Bowen, Jose Antonio, and C. Edward Watson. 2017. *Teaching Naked Techniques: A Practical Guide to Designing Better Classes*. San Francisco: Jossey-Bass.

Briggs, Stephanie. 2018. *Be.Still.Move*. http://www.bestillmove.com.

Bruff, Derek. 2019. *Intentional Tech: Principles to Guide the Use of Educational Technology in College Teaching*. Morgantown: West Virginia University Press.

Busteed, Brandon. 2019. "A Nobel Laureate's Mind-Blowing Perspective on the Ultimate Outcome of an Education." *Education* (blog). *Forbes*. December 23, 2019. https://www.forbes.com/sites/brandonbusteed/2019/12/23/a -nobel-laureates-mind-blowing-perspective-on-the-ultimate-outcome-of-an -education/#547779476cd5.

Cain, Susan. 2012. *Quiet: The Power of Introverts in a World That Can't Stop Talking*. New York: Crown.

Carnes, Mark C. 2014. *Minds on Fire: How Role-Immersion Games Transform College*. Cambridge, MA: Harvard University Press.

Carter, Lauren. 2017. "The Bounce." *November Project* (blog). August 2, 2017. https://november-project.com/the-bounce/.

Cartwright, Benjamin D. S., Mathew P. White, and Theodore J. Clitherow. 2018. "Nearby Nature 'Buffers' the Effect of Low Social Connectedness on Adult Subjective Wellbeing over the Last 7 Days." *International Journal of Environmental Research and Public Health* 15 (6): 1238. https://doi.org/10.3390/ijerph15061238.

Castellanos, Sara. 2019. "A Tech Nerd Walks into a Bar . . . Campus Requires Improv Class for Computer Scientists." *Wall Street Journal*, May 14, 2019. https://www.wsj.com/articles/oh-my-god-where-is-this-going-when-computer-science-majors-take-improv-11557846729.

Causey, Andrew. 2015. "Objects Possessed, Drawn, Touched, Identified, and Sold: Effective Material Culture Exercises for the Anthropology Classroom." *Museum Anthropology* 38 (2): 133–48. https://doi.org/10.1111/muan.12089.

Cavanagh, Sarah Rose. 2015. "10 Reasons You Should Go to Sleep Right Now." *Once More, with Feeling* (blog), *Psychology Today*. March 25, 2015. https://www.psychologytoday.com/us/blog/once-more-feeling/201503/10-reasons-you-should-go-sleep-right-now.

———. 2016. *The Spark of Learning: Energizing the College Classroom with the Science of Emotion*. Morgantown: West Virginia University Press.

Cavanagh, Sarah R., James M. Lang, Jeffrey L. Birk, Carl E. Fulwiler, and Heather L. Urry. 2019. "A Multicourse, Multisemester Investigation of the Impact of Cognitive Reappraisal and Mindfulness Instruction on Short- and Long-Term Learning in the College Classroom." *Scholarship of Teaching and Learning in Psychology*. Advance Online Publication. https://doi.org/10.1037/stl0000174.

Center for Contemplative Mind in Society. 2015. "The Tree of Contemplative Practices." http://www.contemplativemind.org/practices/tree.

Clark, Andy. 2008. *Supersizing the Mind: Embodiment, Action, and Cognitive Extension*. New York: Oxford University Press.

———. 2013. "Whatever Next? Predictive Brains, Situated Agents, and the Future of Cognitive Science." *Behavioral and Brain Sciences* 36 (3): 181–204. http://dx.doi.org/10.1017/S0140525X12000477.

Claxton, Guy. 2015. *Intelligence in the Flesh: Why Your Mind Needs Your Body Much More than It Thinks*. New Haven: Yale University Press.

Clifford, M. Amos. 2018. "Forest Therapy: 8 Steps to Begin." *Association of Nature and Forest Therapy Guides and Programs*. https://www.natureandforesttherapy.org.

Congdon, Christine, Donna Flynn, and Melanie Redman. 2014. "Balancing 'We' and 'Me': The Best Collaborative Spaces Also Support Solitude." *Harvard Business Review* (October). https://hbr.org/2014/10/balancing-we-and-me-the-best-collaborative-spaces-also-support-solitude.

Coppin, Géraldine, Eva Pool, Sylvain Delplanque, Bastiaan Oud, Christian

Margot, David Sander, and Jay J. Van Bavel. 2016. "Swiss Identity Smells Like Chocolate: Social Identity Shapes Olfactory Judgments." *Scientific Reports* 6: 34979. https://doi.org/10.1038/srep34979.

Crawford, Matthew B. 2015. *The World beyond Your Head: On Becoming an Individual in an Age of Distraction*. New York: Farrar, Straus and Giroux.

Cregan-Reid, Vybarr. 2018a. *Primate Change: How the World We Made Is Remaking Us*. London: Octopus.

———. 2018b. "Why We Are Living in the Age of the Chair." *BBC Future*, November 9, 2018. http://www.bbc.com/future/story/20181108-the-anthropocene-should-be-known-as-the-age-of-the-chair.

———. 2019. "Why Exercise Alone Won't Save Us." *The Guardian*, January 3, 2019. https://www.theguardian.com/news/2019/jan/03/why-exercise-alone-wont-save-us.

Cutting, James E. 2013. "Gunnar Johanssen, Events, and Biological Motion." In *People Watching: Social Perceptual, and Neurophysiological Studies of Body Perception*, edited by Kerri L. Johnson and Maggie Schiffrar. New York: Oxford University Press.

Dabke, Rajeev B., and Zewdu Gebeyehu. 2010. "Using Magnets, Paper Clips, and Ball Bearings to Explore Molecular Geometries." *Journal of College Science Teaching* 40 (2): 70–73.

Damasio, Antonio R. 1999. *The Feeling of What Happens: Body and Emotion in the Making of Consciousness*. New York: Harcourt Brace.

Damasio, Antonio R., Barry John Everitt, Dorothy Bishop, A. C. Roberts, Trevor William Robbins, and Lawrence Weiskrantz. 1996. "The Somatic Marker Hypothesis and the Possible Functions of the Prefrontal Cortex." *Philosophical Transactions of the Royal Society B* 351: 1413–20. http://doi.org/10.1098/rstb.1996.0125.

Davidson, Cathy N. 2015. "The Single Best Method for Class (or Any Kind of) Participation (Thx SciFi Genius Samuel Delany)." *Hastac* (blog). February 2, 2015. https://www.hastac.org/blogs/cathy-davidson/2015/02/02/single-best-method-class-or-any-kind-participation-thx-scifi-genius.

Davidson, Richard J., and Sharon Begley. 2012. *The Emotional Life of Your Brain: How Its Unique Patterns Affect the Way You Think, Feel, and Live—and How You Can Change Them*. New York: Hudson Street.

Deng, Huan, and Ping Hu. 2018. "Matching Your Face or Appraising the Situation: Two Paths to Emotional Contagion." *Frontiers in Psychology* 8: 2278. https://doi.org/10.3389/fpsyg.2017.02278.

Depenbrock, Julie. 2017. " 'Nature Preschools' Spread like Weeds." *Education Week* 36 (18): 7.

Desjardins, Jeff. 2017. "Every Single Cognitive Bias in One Infographic." *Visual Capitalist*. Last modified September 25, 2017. https://www.visualcapitalist.com/every-single-cognitive-bias/.

Desteno, David. 2017. "The Only Way to Keep Your Resolutions." *New York Times*, December 29, 2017. https://nyti.ms/2EcudW6.

Dissanayake, Ellen. 2000. *Art and Intimacy: How the Arts Began*. Seattle: University of Washington Press.

Eady, Ashley. 2019. "Body Mapping Helps Musicians." *Music Major* (blog). https://majoringinmusic.com/body-mapping-helps-musicians/.

Ekman, Paul. 2003. *Emotions Revealed*. New York: Times Books.

Engle-Friedman, Mindy, Suzanne Riela, and Elaine Strothers. 2008. "Objective and Subjective Effort as a Function of Sleep and Energy." *Sleep and Hypnosis* 10 (2): 61–72.

Epley, Nicholas, and Juliana Schroeder. 2014. "Mistakenly Seeking Solitude." *Journal of Experimental Psychology* 143 (5): 1980–1999.

Epstein, David. 2019. *Range: Why Generalists Triumph in a Specialized World*. New York: Riverhead.

Eyler, Joshua R. 2018a. " 'Active Learning' Has Become a Buzzword (and Why That Matters)." *Reflections on Teaching and Learning* (blog). July 17, 2018. http://cte.rice.edu/blogarchive/2018/7/16/active-learning-has-become-a-buzz-word.

———. 2018b. *How Humans Learn: The Science and Stories behind Effective College Teaching*. 1st ed. Morgantown: West Virginia University Press.

Fadiman, Anne. 1998. *Ex Libris: Confessions of a Common Reader*. New York: Farrar, Straus, Giroux.

Farias, Joaquin. 2015. "How Your Movements Can Heal Your Brain." Filmed July 13, 2015, in Naples, Italy. TEDxNapoli. https://youtu.be/czW-xBvDtHY.

Fenker, Daniela, and Hartmut Schütze. 2008. "Learning by Surprise." *Scientific American Mind* 19 (6): 47. https://www.jstor.org/stable/24940019.

Figueiro, M. G., and M. S. Rea. 2016. "Office Lighting and Personal Light Exposures in Two Seasons: Impact on Sleep and Mood." *Lighting Research and Technology* 48 (3): 352.

Fiorella, Logan, and Richard E. Mayer. 2015. *Learning as a Generative Activity: Eight Learning Strategies That Promote Understanding*. New York: Cambridge University Press.

Forstmann, Matthias, Pascal Burgmer, and Thomas Mussweiler. 2012. " 'The Mind Is Willing, but the Flesh Is Weak': The Effects of Mind-Body Dualism on Health Behavior." *Psychological Science* 23 (10): 1239–45. doi:10.1177/0956797612442392.

Frijda, Nico H., and Louise Sundararajan. 2007. "Emotion Refinement: A Theory Inspired by Chinese Poetics." *Perspectives on Psychological Science* 2 (3): 227–41. https://doi.org/10.1111/j.1745-6916.2007.00042.x.

Fromm, Erich. 1964. *The Heart of Man: Its Genius for Good and Evil*. 1st ed. New York: Harper and Row.

Gallese, Vittorio. 2004. "The Manifold Nature of Interpersonal Relations: The Quest for a Common Mechanism." In *The Neuroscience of Social Interaction: Decoding, Imitating, and Influencing the Actions of Others*, edited by Christopher D. Frith and Daniel M. Wolpert, 159–82. Oxford: Oxford University Press.

Garfinkel, Sarah N., Anil K. Seth, Adam B. Barrett, Keisuke Suzuki, and Hugo D. Critchley. 2015. "Knowing Your Own Heart: Distinguishing Interoceptive Accuracy from Interoceptive Awareness." *Biological Psychology* 104: 65–74.

Gay, Roxane. 2017. *Hunger: A Memoir of (My) Body*. New York: HarperCollins.

Gaydosh, Lauren, Kristen M. Schorpp, Edith Chen, Gregory E. Miller, and Kathleen Mullan Harris. 2018. "College Completion Predicts Lower Depression but Higher Metabolic Syndrome among Disadvantaged Minorities in Young Adulthood." *Proceedings of the National Academy of Sciences* 115 (1): 109–14. https://doi.org/10.1073/pnas.1714616114.

Genetic Science Learning Center. 2013. "Epigenetics and Inheritance." *Learn. Genetics*. https://learn.genetics.utah.edu/content/epigenetics /inheritance/.

Geronimus, Arline T. 2013. "Deep Integration: Letting the Epigenome Out of the Bottle without Losing Sight of the Structural Origins of Population Health." *American Journal of Public Health* 103 (S1): S56–63. https://doi .org/10.2105/AJPH.2013.301380.

Gervasio, Amy Herstein. 2012. "Toward a Psychology of Responses to Dance Performance." *Research in Dance Education* 13 (3): 257–78.

Gewolb, Josh. 2001. "Surprise Me, Please!" *ScienceNOW* 1 (April 17).

Gilbert, Avery N. 2008. *What the Nose Knows: The Science of Scent in Everyday Life*. New York: Crown.

Giscombe, C. S. 2019. "The Amputee Cyclist's Art of Self-Repair." *New York Times*, May 23, 2019. https://nyti.ms/2VKA9gj.

Gladwell, Malcolm. 2005. *Blink: The Power of Thinking without Thinking*. 1st ed. New York: Little, Brown.

Gracia-Bafalluy, Maria, and Marie-Pascale Noël. 2008. "Does Finger Training Increase Young Children's Numerical Performance?" *Cortex* 44 (4): 368–75. https://doi.org/10.1016/j.cortex.2007.08.020.

Greater Good Science Center, University of California–Berkeley. 2020. "Mindful Breathing." *Greater Good in Action*. https://ggia.berkeley.edu /practice/mindful_breathing.

Gruber, Matthias J., Bernard D. Gelman, and Charan Ranganath. 2014. "States of Curiosity Modulate Hippocampus-Dependent Learning via the Dopaminergic Circuit." *Neuron* 84 (2): 486–96.

Hackel, Leor M., Géraldine Coppin, Michael J. A. Wohl, and Jay J. Van Bavel. 2018. "From Groups to Grits: Social Identity Shapes Evaluations of Food Pleasantness." *Journal of Experimental Social Psychology* 74: 270–80.

Hansen, Anders. 2016. *The Real Happy Pill: Power Up Your Brain by Moving Your Body*. New York: Skyhorse.

Henry, Alan. 2016. "The Benefits of Writing by Hand versus Typing."

LifeHacker. May 18, 2016. https://lifehacker.com/the-benefits-of-writing -by-hand-versus-typing-1778758792.

Hjortshoj, Keith. 2009. *The Transition to College Writing*. 2nd ed. Boston: Bedford/St. Martin's.

Hobson, Nicholas M., Devin Bonk, and Michael Inzlicht. 2017. "Rituals Decrease the Neural Response to Performance Failure." *PeerJ*, e3363. https://doi.org/10.7717/peerj.3363.

Hohwy, Jakob. 2014. *The Predictive Mind*. New York: Oxford University Press.

Holmes, Emma, Ysabel Domingo, and Ingrid S. Johnsrude. 2018. "Familiar Voices Are More Intelligible, Even If They Are Not Recognized as Familiar." *Psychological Science 29* (10): 1575–83. https://doi.org/10.1177/09567976 18779083.

Holton, Doug. 2010. "The Connection between Embodied Cognition and Learning: 3 Examples from Physics Education." *EdTechDev*, March 24, 2010. https://edtechdev.wordpress.com/2010/03/24/the-connection -between-embodied-cognition-and-learning-3-examples-from-physics -education/.

Harari, Yuval Noah. 2015. *Sapiens: A Brief History of Humankind*. New York: Harper.

———. 2016. "Why Did Humans Become the Most Successful Species on Earth?" *TED Radio Hour*. March 4, 2016. https://www.npr.org/2016/03/04 /468882620/why-did-humans-become-the-most-successful-species-on -earth.

Ianes, Dario, Sofia Cramerotti, and Angela Cattoni. 2017. "Embodied Cognition and Special Education." In *Embodied Cognition: Theories and Applications in Education Science*, edited by Filippo Gomez Paloma, 13–48. New York: Nova Science.

Iberall, A. S., and Soodak, H. 1987. "A Physics for Complex Systems." In *Self-Organizing Systems: The Emergence of Order*, edited by F. E. Yates, 499–520. New York: Plenum.

ISE. 2017. "The Reds and Blues of Productivity: RPI Researcher Says Color Can Help Unleash Your Workforce." *ISE: Industrial and Systems Engineering at Work* 49 (6): 18.

Ittyerah, M. 2013. *Hand Preference and Hand Ability: Evidence from Studies in Haptic Cognition*. Amsterdam: John Benjamins.

Jackson, J. S., K. M. Knight, and J. A. Rafferty. 2010. "Race and Unhealthy Behaviors: Chronic Stress, the HPA Axis, and Physical and Mental Health Disparities over the Life Course." *American Journal Public Health* 100: 933–39.

Jaeger, A. J., J. Wiley, and T. Moher. 2016. "Leveling the Playing Field: Grounding Learning with Embedded Simulations in Geoscience." *Cognitive Research: Principles and Implications* 1: 23.

Jasmin, Kyle, and Daniel Casasanto. 2012. "The QWERTY Effect: How Typing

Shapes the Meaning of Words." *Psychonomic Bulletin and Review* 19: 499. https://doi.org/10.3758/s13423-012-0229-7.

Jepma, Marieke, Rinus G. Verdonschot, Henk Van Steenbergen, Serge A. R. B. Rombouts, and Sander Nieuwenhuis. 2012. "Neural Mechanisms Underlying the Induction and Relief of Perceptual Curiosity." *Frontiers in Behavioral Neuroscience*. https://doi.org/10.3389/fnbeh.2012.00005.

Johansson, Gunnar. 1973. "Visual Perception of Biological Motion and a Model for Its Analysis." *Perception and Psychophysics* 14: 201–11.

Johnson, Mark. 1987. *The Body in the Mind: The Bodily Basis of Meaning, Imagination, and Reason*. Chicago: University of Chicago Press.

Junod, Tom. (1998) 2017. "Can You Say . . . Hero?" *Esquire*, April 6, 2017. https://www.esquire.com/entertainment/tv/a27134/can-you-say-hero-esq1198/.

Kabat-Zinn, Jon, and University of Massachusetts Medical Center/ Worcester Stress Reduction Clinic. 1990. *Full Catastrophe Living: Using the Wisdom of Your Body and Mind to Face Stress, Pain, and Illness*. New York: Delacorte Press.

Kaborycha, Lisa. 2016. *A Corresponding Renaissance: Letters Written by Italian Women, 1375–1650*. New York: Oxford University Press.

Kahneman, Daniel. 2011. *Thinking, Fast and Slow*. New York: Farrar, Straus and Giroux.

Kang, Min Jeong, Ming Hsu, Ian M. Krajbich, George Loewenstein, Samuel M. McClure, Joseph Tao-yi Wang, and Colin F. Camerer. 2009. "The Wick in the Candle of Learning: Epistemic Curiosity Activates Reward Circuitry and Enhances Memory." *Psychological Science* 20 (8): 963–73.

Kang, Okim, and Donald Rubin. 2009. "Reverse Linguistic Stereotyping: Measuring the Effect of listener Expectations on Speech Evaluation." *Journal of Language and Social Psychology* 28: 441–56.

Kang, Okim, Donald Rubin, and Stephanie Lindemann. 2015. "Mitigating U.S. Undergraduates' Attitudes toward International Teaching Assistants." *TESOL Quarterly* 49 (4): 681–706.

Kelly, Scott. 2017. *Endurance: A Year in Space, a Lifetime of Discovery*. New York: Knopf.

Khalid, Saara, Jason C. Deska, and Kurt Hugenberg. 2016. "The Eyes Are the Windows to the Mind: Direct Eye Gaze Triggers the Ascription of Others' Minds." *Personality and Social Psychology Bulletin* 42 (12): 1666–77. https://doi.org/10.1177/0146167216669124.

Kinman, Gail. 2014. "Interview: The Accidental Academic." *Psychologist* 27 (5): 346–48. https://thepsychologist.bps.org.uk/volume-27/edition-5/interview-accidental-academic.

Kircanski, Katharina, Matthew D. Lieberman, and Michelle G. Craske. 2012. "Feelings into Words: Contributions of Language to Exposure Therapy." *Psychological Science* 23 (10): 1086–91.

Kleckner, Ian R., Jiahe Zhang, Alexandra Touroutoglou, Lorena Chanes, Chenjie Xia, W. Kyle Simmons, Karen S. Quigley, Bradford C. Dickerson, Lisa Feldman Barrett. 2017. "Evidence for a Large-Scale Brain System Supporting Allostasis and Interoception in Humans." *Nature Human Behavior* 1 (0069). https://doi.org/10.1038/s41562-017-0069.

Krueger, Joel W. 2009. "Empathy and the Extended Mind." *Zygon: Journal of Religion and Science* 44 (3): 675–98.

Kuepper-Tetzel, Carolina. 2019. "New Findings Inform the Laptop versus Longhand Note-Taking Debate." *The Learning Scientists* (blog). February 21, 2019. http://www.learningscientists.org/blog/2019/2/21-1.

Kuh, George D., and Carol Geary Schneider. 2008. *High-Impact Educational Practices: What They Are, Who Has Access to Them, and Why They Matter*. Washington, DC: Association of American Colleges and Universities.

Kunstman, Jonathan W., Elise M. Clerkin, Katelyn Palmer, M. Taylar Peters, Dorian R. Dodd, and April R. Smith. 2016. "The Power Within: The Experimental Manipulation of Power Interacts with Trait BDD Symptoms to Predict Interoceptive Accuracy." *Journal of Behavior Therapy and Experimental Psychiatry* 50: 178–86. https://doi.org/10.1016/j.jbtep.2015.08.003.

Lakoff, George. 2012. "Explaining Embodied Cognition Results." *Topics in Cognitive Science* 4 (4): 773–85. https://doi.org/10.1111/j.1756-8765.2012.01222.x.

Lang, James M. 2016. *Small Teaching: Everyday Lessons from the Science of Learning*. San Francisco: Jossey-Bass.

Lederbogen, Florian, Peter Kirsch, Leila Haddad, Fabian Streit, Heike Tost, Philipp Schuch, Stefan Wüst, Jens C. Pruessner, Marcella Rietschel, Michael Deuschle, and Andreas Meyer-Lindenberg. 2011. "City Living and Urban Upbringing Affect Neural Social Stress Processing in Humans." *Nature* 474 (7352): 498–501. https://doi.org/10.1038/nature10190.

Lees, S. J., and F. W. Booth. 2004. "Sedentary Death Syndrome." *Canadian Journal of Applied Physiology* 29 (4): 447–60.

Levitt, Steven D., and Stephen J. Dubner. 2005. *Freakonomics: A Rogue Economist Explores the Hidden Side of Everything*. 1st ed. New York: William Morrow.

Levy, Nat. 2017. "The Secret Science of Your Office Space: How Architects Are Using Neuroscience to Make Workers Healthier and More Productive." *GeekWire*, March 21, 2017.

Lewis, C., and Peter J. Lovatt. 2013. "Breaking Away from Set Patterns of Thinking: Improvisation and Divergent Thinking." *Thinking Skills and Creativity* 9: 46–58.

Li, Qing. 2012. *Forest Medicine: Environmental Health—Physical, Chemical and Biological Factors*. New York: Nova Science.

Losonczy-Marshall, Marta, and P. Douglas Marshall. 2013. "Factors in

Students' Seat Selection: An Exploratory Study." *Psychological Reports* 112 (2): 651–66. doi:10.2466/11.07.PR0.112.2.651-666.

Louv, Richard. 2005. *Last Child in the Woods: Saving Our Children from Nature-Deficit Disorder*. 1st ed. Chapel Hill, NC: Algonquin Books of Chapel Hill.

Lovatt, Peter. 2018. *Dance Psychology: The Science of Dance and Dancers*. Norfolk, UK: Dr. Dance Presents.

Lupyan, Gary, and Emily J. Ward. 2013. "Language Can Boost Otherwise Unseen Objects into Visual Awareness." *Proceedings of the National Academy of Sciences* 110 (35): 14196–14201. https://doi.org/10.1073/pnas.1303312110.

Macedonia, Manuela, and Katharina von Kriegstein. 2012. "Gestures Enhance Foreign Language Learning." *Biolinguistics* 6 (3–4): 393–416.

Majid, Asifa, Seán G. Roberts, Ludy Cilissen, Karen Emmorey, Brenda Nicodemus, Lucinda O'Grady, Bencie Woll, Barbara LeLan, Hilário de Sousa, Brian L. Cansler, Shakila Shayan, Connie de Vos, Gunter Senft, N. J. Enfield, Rogayah A. Razak, Sebastian Fedden, Sylvia Tufvesson, MarkDingemanse, Ozge Ozturk, Penelope Brown, Clair Hill, Olivier Le Guen, Vincent Hirtzel, Rik van Gijn, Mark A. Sicoli, and Stephen C. Levinson. 2018. "Differential Coding of Perception in the World's Languages." *Proceedings of the National Academy of Sciences* 115 (45): 11369–76. https://doi.org/10.1073/pnas.1720419115.

Mandsager, Kyle, Serge Harb, Paul Cremer, Dermot Phelan, Steven E. Nissen, and Wael Jaber. 2018. "Association of Cardiorespiratory Fitness with Long-Term Mortality among Adults Undergoing Exercise Treadmill Testing." *JAMA Network Open* 1(6):e183605. https://doi.org/10.1001/jamanetworkopen.2018.3605.

Marsh, Kerry L. 2013. "Coordinating Social Beings in Motion." In *People Watching: Social, Perceptual and Neurophysiological Studies of Body Perception*, edited by Kerri L. Johnson and Maggie Schiffrar, 234–55. Oxford: Oxford University Press.

Marsh, Kerry L., Lucy Johnston, Michael J. Richardson, and R. C. Schmidt. 2009. "Toward a Radically Embodied, Embedded Social Psychology." *European Journal of Social Psychology* 39 (7): 1217–25. https://doi.org/10.1002/ejsp.666.

Mazur, Eric. 1997. *Peer Instruction: A User's Manual*. Upper Saddle River, NJ: Prentice Hall.

McCabe, Ciara, Edmund T. Rolls, Amy Bilderbeck, and Francis McGlone. 2008. "Cognitive Influences on the Affective Representation of Touch and the Sight of Touch in the Human Brain." *Social Cognitive and Affective Neuroscience* 3 (2): 97–108. https://doi.org/10.1093/scan/nsn005.

McCullers, Carson. 1940. *The Heart Is a Lonely Hunter*. Boston: Houghton Mifflin.

McEwen, Bruce S. 2016. "In Pursuit of Resilience: Stress, Epigenetics, and

Brain Plasticity." *Annals of the New York Academy of Sciences* 1373 (1): 56–64. doi:10.1111/nyas.13020.

McMurtrie, Beth. 2019. " 'Brilliant' Philosophers and 'Funny' Psychology Instructors: What a Data-Visualization Tool Tells Us about How Students See Their Professors." Teaching Newsletter, *Chronicle of Higher Education*. November 14, 2019. https://www.chronicle.com/article/Brilliant -Philosophers/247523.

Mehling, W. 2016. "Differentiating Attention Styles and Regulatory Aspects of Self-Reported Interoceptive Sensibility." *Philosophical Transactions of the Royal Society B* 371: 20160013. http://dx.doi.org/10.1098/rstb.2016 .0013.

Mehta, Ranjana K., Ashley E. Shortz, and Mark E. Benden. 2016. "Standing Up for Learning: A Pilot Investigation on the Neurocognitive Benefits of Stand-Biased School Desks." *International Journal of Environmental Research and Public Health* 13:59. https://doi.org/10.3390/ijerph130 10059.

Meyers-Levy, Joan, and Rui (Juliet) Zhu. 2007. "The Influence of Ceiling Height: The Effect of Priming on the Type of Processing That People Use." *Journal of Consumer Research* 2: 174.

Moore-Russo, Deborah, Francesca Ferrara, and Laurie D. Edwards. 2014. *Emerging Perspectives on Gesture and Embodiment in Mathematics.* Charlotte, NC: Information Age.

Moore, Glenn. 2013. *Searching for the American Dream: How a Sense of Place Shapes the Study of History.* Newcastle upon Tyne, GB: Cambridge Scholars.

Mullainathan, Sendhil, and Eldar Shafir. 2013. *Scarcity: The New Science of Having Less and How It Defines Our Lives.* New York: Picador.

Mussweiler, Thomas. 2006. "Doing Is for Thinking! Stereotype Activation by Stereotypic Movements." *Psychological Science* 17 (1): 17. https://www .jstor.org/stable/40064344.

Narum, Jeanne L. 2011. "From Audits to Quick Fixes: Critical Questions." *Learning Spaces Collaboratory.* https://www.pkallsc.org/resources/audits -quick-fixes-critical-questions/.

National Disability Authority. 2014. "The 7 Principles." *What Is Universal Design.* Centre for Excellence in Universal Design. http://universaldesign .ie/What-is-Universal-Design/.

Norton, Michael I., Daniel Mochon, and Dan Ariely. 2012. "The IKEA Effect: When Labor Leads to Love." *Journal of Consumer Psychology* 22 (3): 453–60. https://doi.org/10.1016/j.jcps.2011.08.002.

Opel, Nils, Stella Martin, Susanne Meinert, Ronny Redlich, Verena Enneking, Maike Richter, Janik Goltermann, Andreas Johnen, Udo Dannlowski, and Jonathan Repple. 2019. "White Matter Microstructure Mediates the Association between Physical Fitness and Cognition in Healthy, Young

Adults." *Scientific Reports* 9 (12885). https://doi.org/10.1038/s41598 -019-49301-y.

Osher Center for Integrative Medicine. 2018. "Multidimensional Assessment of Interoceptive Awareness v2." University of California San Francisco. https://osher.ucsf.edu/sites/osher.ucsf.edu/files/inline-files/MAIA-2.pdf.

Owen-Smith, Patricia. 2018. *The Contemplative Mind in the Scholarship of Teaching and Learning*. Bloomington: Indiana University Press.

Ozenc, Kurzat, and Margaret Hagan. 2019. *Rituals for Work: 50 Ways to Create Engagement, Shared Purpose and a Culture That Can Adapt to Change*. Hoboken, NJ: John Wiley and Sons.

Palagi, Elisabetta, Velia Nicotra, and Giada Cordoni. 2015. "Rapid Mimicry and Emotional Contagion in Domestic Dogs." *Royal Society Open Science* 2 (12): 150505. https://doi.org/10.1098/rsos.150505.

Pasanen, Tytti P., Liisa Tyrväinen, and Kalevi M. Korpela. 2014. "The Relationship between Perceived Health and Physical Activity Indoors, Outdoors in Built Environments, and Outdoors in Nature." *Applied Psychology: Health and Well-Being* 6 (3): 324–46. https://doi.org/10.1111 /aphw.12031.

Perkins, Katherine K., and Carl E. Wieman. 2005. "The Surprising Impact of Seat Location on Student Performance." *Physics Teacher* 43 (1): 30. https:// doi.org/10.1119/1.1845987.

Pollan, Michael. 2018. *How to Change Your Mind: What the New Science of Psychedelics Teaches Us about Consciousness, Dying, Addiction, Depression, and Transcendence*. New York: Penguin.

Ramachandran, V. S. 2008. "Illusions: Seeing Is Believing." *Scientific American Mind* 19 (4): 16–18. https://doi.org/10.1038/scientificamericanmind 0808-16.

Ramachandran, V. S., and Sandra Blakeslee. 1998. *Phantoms in the Brain: Probing the Mysteries of the Human Mind*. New York: Williams Morrow.

Rands, Melissa L., and Ann M. Gansemer-Topf. 2017. "The Room Itself Is Active: How Classroom Design Impacts Student Engagement." *Journal of Learning Spaces* 6 (1): 26–33.

Rasch, Björn, Christian Büchel, Steffen Gais, and Jan Born. 2007. "Odor Cues during Slow-Wave Sleep Prompt Declarative Memory Consolidation." *Science* 315 (5817): 1426–29. https://doi.org/10.1126/science.1138581.

Ratey, John J., and Eric Hagerman. 2008. *Spark: The Revolutionary New Science of Exercise and the Brain*. New York: Little, Brown.

Ratey, John J., Richard Manning, and David Perlmutter. 2014. *Go Wild: Eat Fat, Run Free, Be Social, and Follow Evolution's Other Rules for Total Health and Well-Being*. New York: Little, Brown.

Rhodes Trust. 2019. "Could You Be a Rhodes Scholar?" Rhodes Scholarship. https://www.rhodeshouse.ox.ac.uk/scholarships/the-rhodes-scholarship/.

Rifkin, Jeremy. 2009. *The Empathic Civilization: The Race to Global Consciousness in a World in Crisis*. New York: J. P. Tarcher/Penguin.

Rittell, Horst, and Melvin Webber. 1973. "Dilemmas in a General Theory of Planning." *Policy Sciences* 4: 155–69.

Rocchesso, Davide, Stefania Serafin, and Michal Rinott. 2013. "Pedagogical Approaches and Methods." In *Sonic Interaction Design*, edited by Stefania Serafin and Karmen Franinović, chapter 4. Cambridge, MA: MIT Press.

Rosling, Hans, Ola Rönnlund, Ola Rosling, and Anna Rosling Rönnlund. 2018. *Factfulness: Ten Reasons We're Wrong about the World and Why Things Are Better than You Think*. 1st ed. New York: Flat Iron.

Saarela, Miiamaaria V., and Riitta Hari. 2008. "Listening to Humans Walking Together Activates the Social Brain Circuitry." *Social Neuroscience* 3 (3/4): 401–9. https://doi.org/10.1080/17470910801897633.

Sacks, Oliver. 2019. "Oliver Sacks: The Healing Power of Gardens." Opinion. *New York Times*, April 18, 2019. https://www.nytimes.com/2019/04/18 /opinion/sunday/oliver-sacks-gardens.html.

Santos, Laurie. *The Science of Well-Being*. 2018. Yale University. https://www .coursera.org/learn/the-science-of-well-being?.

Sapolsky, Robert M. 2017. *Behave: The Biology of Humans at Our Best and Worst*. New York: Penguin Press.

Schnall, Simone, Kent Harber, Jeanine Stefanucci, and Dennis Proffitt. 2008. "Social Support and the Perception of Geographical Slant." *Journal of Experimental Social Psychology* 44: 1246–55. https://doi.org/10.1016/j .jesp.2008.04.011.

Scott-Webber, Lennie, Aileen Strickland, and Laura Ring Kapitula. 2013. "Built Environments Impact Behaviors Results of an Active Learning Post-Occupancy Evaluation." *Planning for Higher Education* 42 (1): 28–39.

Selingo, Jeffrey. 2018. "The Future of the Faculty Office." Steelcase Education. https://www.steelcase.com/content/uploads/2018/04/Future _of_Faculty_Office.pdf.

Seth, A. K. 2013. "Interoceptive Inference, Emotion, and the Embodied Self." *Trends in Cognitive Sciences* 17 (11): 656–63. http://www.sciencedirect .com/science/article/pii/S1364661313002118.

———. 2017. "Your Brain Hallucinates Your Conscious Reality." *TED2017*. https://www.ted.com/talks/anil_seth_your_brain_hallucinates_your _conscious_reality.

Seth, Anil K., and Manos Tsakiris. 2018. "Being a Beast Machine: The Somatic Basis of Selfhood." *Trends in Cognitive Sciences* 22 (11): 969–81. https://doi.org/10.1016/j.tics.2018.08.008.

Shaw, Kimberly A., and Chloe A. Chambers. 2017. "Determining What Factors Dictate STEM Student Retention." *Interdisciplinary STEM Teaching and Learning Conference*, 42. https://digitalcommons.georgia southern.edu/stem/2017/2017/42.

Shining Red Productions, Inc. 2015. *E. O. Wilson—Of Ants and Men*. Premiered on PBS September 30, 2015.

Siddarth, Prabha, Alison C. Burggren, Harris A. Eyre, Gary W. Small, and

David A. Merrill. 2018. "Sedentary Behavior Associated with Reduced Medial Temporal Lobe Thickness in Middle-Aged and Older Adults." *PLOS ONE*, April 12, 2018. https://doi.org/10.1371/journal.pone.0195549.

Siegel, Daniel J. 2006. Series editor's foreword. In *Trauma and the Body: A Sensorimotor Approach to Psychotherapy*, edited by Pat Ogden, Kakuni Minton, and Claire Pain. New York: W. W. Norton.

Siegel, Erika H., Jolie B. Wormwood, Karen S. Quigley, and Lisa Feldman Barrett. 2018. "Seeing What You Feel: Affect Drives Visual Perception of Structurally Neutral Faces." *Psychological Science* 29 (4): 496–503. http://journals.sagepub.com/doi/suppl/10.1177/0956797617741718.

Simons, Daniel. 2012. "But Did You See the Gorilla? The Problem with Inattentional Blindness." *Smithsonian Magazine*. September 2012. https://www.smithsonianmag.com/science-nature/but-did-you-see-the-gorilla-the-problem-with-inattentional-blindness-17339778/.

Sims, David. 2018. "*They Shall Not Grow Old* is a Stunning World War I Documentary." *Culture* (blog), *The Atlantic*. December 19, 2018. https://www.theatlantic.com/entertainment/archive/2018/12/peter-jackson-they-shall-not-grow-old-world-war-i-documentary/578542/.

Smith, David P., Angela Hoare, and Melissa M. Lacey. 2018. "Who Goes Where? The Importance of Peer Groups on Attainment and the Student Use of the Lecture Theatre Teaching Space." *FEBS Open Bio* 8: 1368–78.

Song, Chorong, Harumi Ikei, and Yoshifumi Miyazaki. 2016. "Physiological Effects of Nature Therapy: A Review of the Research in Japan." *International Journal of Environmental Research and Public Health* 13 (8). https://doi.org/10.3390/ijerph13080781.

Spehar, Branka, Colin W. G. Clifford, Ben R. Newell, and Richard P. Taylor. 2003. "Chaos and Graphics: Universal Aesthetic of Fractals." *Computers and Graphics* 27 (5): 813–20. https://doi.org/10.1016/S0097-8493(03)00154-7.

Spelman College. 2019. "Beverly Daniel Tatum." https://www.spelman.edu/about-us/office-of-the-president/past-presidents/beverly-daniel-tatum.

Stanford SPARQ. 2018. "SPARQ Health Director Crum Discusses Mindsets at the World Economic Forum." *SPARQ: Social Psychological Answers to Real-World Questions*. https://sparq.stanford.edu/sparq-health-director-crum-discusses-mindsets-world-economic-forum-video.

Starr, G. Gabrielle. 2013. *Feeling Beauty: The Neuroscience of Aesthetic Experience*. Cambridge: MIT Press.

Steelcase. 2018. "Tomorrow's Classroom with Educator Jeff Selingo." 360 Research Podcasts. https://www.steelcase.com/research/podcasts/topics/education/tomorrows-classroom-educator-jeff-selingo/.

———. n.d. "Active Learning Centers Impact Education." Steelcase 360 Research. Accessed September 5, 2018. https://www.steelcase.com

/research/articles/topics/classroom-design/impact-on-education-in-active-learning-centers/.

———. n.d. "The Effects of a Stimulating Learning Environment." Steelcase 360 Research. Accessed September 5, 2018. https://www.steelcase.com/research/articles/topics/classroom-design/effects-stimulating-learning-environment/.

Sterling, P., and J. Eyer. 1988. "Allostasis: A New Paradigm to Explain Arousal Pathology." In *Handbook of Life Stress, Cognition and Health*, edited by S. Fisher & J. Reason, 629–49. New York: John Wiley and Sons.

Strickland, Bill. 2018. "The Art of Leadership and the Business of Social Change." Jim Blanchard Leadership Forum, Columbus, GA. August 27, 2018.

Tam, Cheung On. 2015. "Three Cases of Using Object-Based Learning with University Students: A Comparison of their Rationales, Impact and Effectiveness." In *Engaging the Senses: Object-Based Learning in Higher Education*, edited by Helen J. Chatterjee and Leonie Hannan. Burlington, VT: Ashgate.

Taylor, Richard. 2002. "Science in Culture." *Nature* 415 (6875): 961.

Terrapin Bright Green. 2014. "14 Patterns of Biophilic Design: Improving Health and Well-Being in the Built Environment." https://www.terrapinbrightgreen.com/report/14-patterns/.

Toscano, Pasquale S. 2017. "The Myth of Disability 'Sob-Stories.' " *New York Times*, June 14, 2017. https://www.nytimes.com/2017/06/14/opinion/the-myth-of-disability-sob-stories.html.

Tverysky, Barbara. 2019. *Mind in Motion: How Action Shapes Thought*. New York: Basic.

Uhl, Christopher, and Dana Stuchul. 2011. *Teaching as If Life Matters: The Promise of a New Education Culture*. Baltimore, MD: Johns Hopkins University Press.

Ulrich, Roger S. 1984. "View through a Window May Influence Recovery from Surgery." *Science* 224 (4647): 420–21. https://doi.org/10.1126/science.6143402.

Van Rompay, T., P. Hekkert, and W. Muller. 2005. "The Bodily Basis of Product Experience." *Design Studies* 26 (4): 359–77.

Verschelden, Cia. 2017. *Bandwidth Recovery: Helping Students Reclaim Cognitive Resources Lost to Poverty, Racism, and Social Marginalization*. Sterling, VA: Stylus.

Walker, Matthew. 2017. *Why We Sleep: Unlocking the Power of Sleep and Dreams*. New York: Scribner.

Wallace, B. A. 2006. *The Attention Revolution: Unlocking the Power of the Focused Mind*. Boston: Wisdom.

Wallner, Peter, Michael Kundi, Arne Arnberger, Renate Eder, Brigitte

Allex, Lisbeth Weitensfelder, and Hans-Peter Hutter. 2018. "Reloading Pupils' Batteries: Impact of Green Spaces on Cognition and Wellbeing." *International Journal of Environmental Research and Public Health* 15 (6). https://doi.org/10.3390/ijerph15061205.

Weineck, Felicitas, Matthias Messner, Gernot Hauke, and Olga Pollatos. 2019. "Improving Interoceptive Ability through the Practice of Power Posing: A Pilot Study." *PLOS ONE* 14 (2): e0211453. https://doi.org/10.1371/journal.pone.0211453.

Wendel, Monica L., Mark E. Benden, Zhao Hongwei, and Christina Jeffrey. 2016. "Stand-Biased versus Seated Classrooms and Childhood Obesity: A Randomized Experiment in Texas." *American Journal of Public Health* 106 (10): 1849–54.

Wesch, Michael. 2018. "ANTH 101 Students: Transformative Experiences." Filmed July 2017 in Kansas City, MO. YouTube. https://youtu.be/A1clegYOlg4.

Whitehouse, Bonnie Smith. 2019. *Afoot and Lighthearted: A Journal for Mindful Walking*. New York: Clarkson Potter.

Whiteley, Greg, dir. 2015. *Most Likely to Succeed*. One Potato Productions.

Wick, Katharina, Faude Oliver, Manes Susanne, Zahner Lukas, and Donath Lars. 2018. "I Can Stand Learning: A Controlled Pilot Intervention Study on the Effects of Increased Standing Time on Cognitive Function in Primary School Children." *International Journal of Environmental Research and Public Health* 15 (2): 356.

Williams, Florence. 2017. *The Nature Fix: Why Nature Makes Us Happier, Healthier, and More Creative*. New York: W. W. Norton.

Wilson, Edward O. *Biophilia*. 1984. Cambridge, MA: Harvard University Press.

Wolpert, Daniel M. 2011. "The Real Reason for Brains." *TEDGlobal*. https://www.ted.com/talks/daniel_wolpert_the_real_reason_for_brains.

Yang, Lin, Chao Cao, Elizabeth D. Kantor, Long H. Nguyen, Xiaobin Zheng, Yikyung Park, Edward L. Giovannucci, Charles E. Matthews, Graham A. Colditz, and Yin Cao. 2019. "Trends in Sedentary Behavior among the US Population, 2001–2016." *JAMA* 321 (16): 1587–97. https://doi.org/10.1001/jama.2019.3636.

Zinn, Howard. 2005. *On Democratic Education*. Boulder, CO: Paradigm.

Zull, James E. 2011. *From Brain to Mind: Using Neuroscience to Guide Change in Education*. 1st ed. Sterling, VA: Stylus.

INDEX

. . . .

Page numbers in italics refer to figures.

TEACHING AND LEARNING IN HIGHER EDUCATION

Ungrading: Why Rating Students Undermines Learning
(and What to Do Instead)
Edited by Susan D. Blum

Radical Hope: A Teaching Manifesto
Kevin M. Gannon

Teaching about Race and Racism in the College Classroom:
Notes from a White Professor
Cyndi Kernahan

Intentional Tech: Principles to Guide the Use of Educational
Technology in College Teaching
Derek Bruff

Geeky Pedagogy: A Guide for Intellectuals, Introverts,
and Nerds Who Want to Be Effective Teachers
Jessamyn Neuhaus

How Humans Learn: The Science and Stories
behind Effective College Teaching
Joshua R. Eyler

Reach Everyone, Teach Everyone: Universal Design
for Learning in Higher Education
Thomas J. Tobin and Kirsten T. Behling

Teaching the Literature Survey Course:
New Strategies for College Faculty
Gwynn Dujardin, James M. Lang, and John A. Staunton

The Spark of Learning:
Energizing the College Classroom with the Science of Emotion
Sarah Rose Cavanagh